D1596826

Bur Mousbery

2009

[handwritten inscription, illegible signature] 2009

NEVER GIVE UP

James Harrison Has Conquered Hardship and Daunting Odds To Become One of the Great Pittsburgh Steeler Linebackers

By Bill Moushey with Bill Parise

Parmoush Publishing
Pennsylvania

Published by Parmoush Publishing, 1519 Bluestone Drive, Glenshaw, Pa. 15116,
Bmoushey@pointpark.edu, Sports Management & Marketing Inc. (smmi@aol.com),
and/or www.jamesharrisonnevergiveup.com.

Other products:
The Silverback Package – $45.95 for a signed edition
The Ultimate Harrison – $92.92 for a signed book and signed, framed glossy reprint of the cover
The E-Book – $12.95
The Eaudio Book – $14.95

Printed in the United States of America
Design by Catherine Tigano Gianella
Edited by Peter Leo
Copy editor: Helen Fallon
Cover photograph copyrighted by the Pittsburgh Post-Gazette
Reprinted with permission

Library of Congress Control Number: 2009908771
Library of Congress Cataloging-in-publication Data
ISBN 978-0-9842049-0-8
First Edition

To my adorable wife Kristine, my loving children,
Wil and Leah, not only for their unconditional love but for
making room in their lives for me to do the work I cherish,
and to dear old dad, who is still kicking at 88.
– Bill Moushey

To all the athletes who have allowed
me the pleasure of sharing their dreams
and helping to make them a reality.

To James Harrison for giving me the privilege
of being part of one of the greatest stories in sports
and helping me to remember to never give up.

To Linda, who has cared as much as I have
and shown me the meaning of love.
—Bill Parise

CONTENTS

CONTENTS

PROLOGUE

A first encounter with James Harrison is a daunting proposition for most. His sullen, menacing look makes him appear to be one tough hombre. But intimidation has never worked on me. Maybe it's because of my own upbringing as a jock, where anyone who succumbed to threats and intimidation was cast aside as weak.

There was nothing in his past that unsettled me. In Canton, Ohio, in the 1970s, I faced off against the same kinds of football players James Harrison, who grew up in nearby Akron, played against in high school and college two decades later. Talk about intimidation. As a walk-on kicker at Kent State, I had to tackle Jack Lambert in practice, which quickly helped me to realize I'd be much better off writing about people than hitting them . . . or letting them hit me.

During 30 years in the trenches of street journalism, I've had anxious moments in shaky places with my share of "bad guys." I've faced down menacing hoods in Brooklyn, mob mainstays in Queens, people lurking on the dark streets of Miami's Liberty City or in dank prison visiting rooms, among many uncomfortable interviews.

There were back-room interviews with mob bosses from Ohio, Western Pennsylvania and New York. There were more than 150 people in the federal witness protection program who tried to impose their will on me to no avail.

People often ask if I was ever threatened, and I'd say yes, but "no reputable bad guy is going to tell you he's going to kill you. They'll just do it."

I didn't even flinch while writing stories about drug cartel members from South America, who would sooner shoot reporters than look at them. Maybe it was because I wrote mostly about cartel figures who were locked up, even if they had plenty of foot soldiers on the outside who could have done me in. Or maybe I was just not smart enough to be afraid.

So I was not exactly overcome with anxiety when I drove through winding North Hills streets to Harrison's abode just weeks after he set a Super Bowl record for the longest interception return for a touchdown. I knew he wasn't exactly talkative. I also knew his reputation with reporters was at best curt and distant.

I thought I'd break the ice by telling Harrison about the hangover I had the day after Super Bowl XLIII, brought on by his 100-yard touchdown romp just before the half. That play caused me and my boys to start swilling shots of Crown Royal as if it were water.

Harrison's response: nothing.

I'll never forget that first interview, as he sat on his couch casually watching a "Norbert" movie, while pages and pages of questions rolled off my tongue. The answers came quickly but were usually not more than a few words.

Listening to the tape later, I realized I talked more than Harrison did. It was a horrible interview, easily my worst ever. He was clearly not comfortable with me, didn't trust me. It was not even apparent that he wanted to tell his story. Maybe Harrison's agent and confidant, Bill Parise, had pushed him into something he didn't want to do.

Parise had told me how Harrison sometimes agreed to public events but backed off because of shyness and his aversion toward large crowds, even when autograph signings and the like could command $20,000 or more for a few hours.

I knew what some of my sports reporter buddies had said about non-interviews they had had with the star linebacker. Even my son the college football player was wary after he mentioned to some Steelers he worked out with that his dad was doing a book on Harrison. "I'll bet that's a good interview," one of them said in jest.

For a while, it seemed they were right. Harrison would answer any question I asked, but he didn't volunteer anything. So with the help of Parise and others, I began to adhere to the old law-yer's adage of knowing the answer to a question before you ask it, hoping to break into "James's" world. As time went on during the spring of 2009, he began to see I was carefully tracking his life, talking to everyone I could find who had a role in it, good or bad. I certainly wasn't going away.

The breakthrough began when I decided to meet his family in its Noah Avenue homestead in West Akron. Harrison's dour na-ture, people said, was a direct "gift" from his mother, who they said could be exceedingly charming or deadly combative, some-times within the same few minutes.

With Parise's help, I made an appointment with Mildred and James Sr. in late February while they were still basking in their son's Super Bowl glory. The flowers helped, with Mildred say-ing "you shouldn't have," when I knew I most assuredly should have.

Then, as I began to unfold what I knew from public records and interviews about the pitfalls and pratfalls her son had endured on his path to stardom, Mildred and Jay, as his father is known, realized I knew what they knew – this was a story that nobody could match.

Of course, there was the trust issue. Mildred made no bones about the fact that she did not trust white people. She had faced racism from the time she was born and didn't appreciate any of it. After a harangue about the constant racial injustice she faced (James Sr. chimed in that she once "quit three jobs in one day" over it), I sat back in their comfortable family room and peered into the woman's eyes as only a red-faced white man of mon-grel European descent could and said: "I'm sure glad I'm not white."

That Mildred laugh – loud, heartfelt and endearing – led me to believe I was finally entering her inner sanctum, even if only for a brief visit. But would James ever open up?

As time went on, she and James Sr. shared many personal stories about raising kids in tough West Akron. Her iron hand left me more worried about what Mildred would do if she didn't like my work than I ever felt about her son. As Parise had told me, her world was different from ours, but it worked for her and her brood.

Mildred proved to be a wonderful, insightful street philosopher whose thoughts about life and raising kids might not be found in Dr. Spock but nevertheless were good enough to keep her kids off the streets, out of jail and beholden to nothing more than a taste of good booze.

Through all her bluster, when one pierced through to her heart, a glow emerged. The same goes for her husband, and I would find later, her youngest child. After weeks of interviewing people all over America, I went back to Harrison for confirmation, denials, embellishment or simply comments.

There were nice things, bad things, too, like his arrest and his dog's attack on his baby son he certainly didn't have any great desire to discuss. But it was clear Harrison – whether it was prodding by his agent or his mother or both – was now at a point where he would answer my questions without flinching.

While I was initially taken aback by his gruff demeanor, as we waded through hours and hours of issues about his life, the edge started to soften. Behind it was a thoughtful, cheerful, analytical person. I also discovered he has one trait that could have caused him to put that shield up in the first place. It might have been his mother's longstanding admonition that only the strong survive on the street, that to display your inner thoughts to anyone is a prescription for disaster.

Then there was another Harrison trait that worked to my advantage: When confronted with facts, however uncomfortable, Harrison faces them, good or bad. If it happened, he'll admit it. If he did it, he takes the blame. If he didn't, he won't tell on anyone to get himself off the hook. He has few regrets about most things too. That's not to say he won't give a blustery dissertation on any of the above.

For me, the falling of the shield was a welcome breath of fresh air. After years of covering bad guys, politicians and others dedicated to hiding the truth, here was a guy who didn't run from it, good, bad or indifferent. While his teammates wondered jokingly if he said anything during interviews, once I pierced his shield, Harrison proved to be a smart, engaging man that few people – even some teammates – had ever seen.

I'm happy to have been given a brief glimpse of his life and to write it. I'm happy to have met his family. I treasure one of my last meetings with him after he spent hours plodding through the text of this book, picking out minor errors and straightening out miniscule discrepancies that only someone who cared would do. At the end of the day, the man who has made millions because he exhibits maximum effort on the field of play and in the weight room thanked me for my efforts in writing what he called "an interesting book." The brief endorsement was not what I expected but happily accepted. I hope you will find it worthy of note, too. While I did get a brief visit into the world of James Harrison, I'm also pretty certain if I ever see him on the street, that shield will probably be back up. At best, he'll probably nod my way, with little more than a "What up?" as he passes by.

For me, that is enough.

NEVER GIVE UP

1

The Longest Yards

Kurt Warner was moving the Arizona Cardinals down the field with ease as seconds ticked away toward halftime of Super Bowl XLIII, with the Steelers up 10-7. The seasoned vet, already a Super Bowl winner, was having no trouble finding ways to avoid Pittsburgh's vaunted zone blitz.

One play, he would dump a pass to the outside before the fast-charging Steeler defense could get to him. The next, he'd go inside, with equal success. For two-time all-pro linebacker James Harrison, Warner's surgical precision was intensely frustrating. "It was like we were always a step late," he would say later.

With 18 seconds left, the Cardinal quarterback stood at the Steelers' 5-yard line, intent on finishing what could have been a back-breaking drive to catapult Arizona into the lead. Harrison was supposed to blitz, but his instincts kicked in. It was time to gamble.

As the reigning NFL Defensive Player of the Year coiled his barely 6-foot frame into a two-point stance, he knew teammate Lawrence Timmons would be coming hard on his left in an all-out blitz. But with the snap of the ball, instead of engaging the monstrous lineman opposite him as the play was designed, Har-

James Harrison tackles Curtis Martin, the Pittsburgh native and Pitt grad, during a game in 2004 when he was filling in for an injured Clark Haggans.

rison dropped back to protect his side of the goal line in case the Cardinal quarterback tried to hit a receiver on an inside slant pattern. His reasoning was solid: The Cards couldn't risk getting caught in bounds with time running out and no timeouts.

Warner saw the blitz, and quickly tossed the ball toward the goal line in the direction of wide receiver Anquan Boldin. He found someone else. In fact, it looked like Harrison was the intended receiver, and Warner would later admit he never saw him. But the interception was only the beginning of what would become one of the most memorable plays in Super Bowl history.

"Sometimes you win and sometimes you lose," he said later of the gamble, adding jokingly that it probably caused his coaches to scream, "No, no, no ... great play!" In reality, Dick LeBeau, defensive coordinator, was elated simply that the Steelers would go to halftime with a lead as he saw Harrison's black helmet moving down the field. His first thought: "Oh, man, I was hoping he'd get on the ground, because then we're off the field."

Then he saw Harrison breaking into open field while his defensive teammates gathering around him for the historic sprint. In that singular moment, Harrison's small stature (by NFL standards) and his speed would become allies the scouts could not see when they left him undrafted out of college, and when he was cut four times from NFL rosters before sticking with the Steelers. Harrison was quick enough to drop back for the interception, but slow enough for teammates to catch up in time to block as he labored down the field.

Starting a yard deep in the end zone, Harrison's first encountered teammate Deshea Townsend. The speedy veteran cornerback grabbed at the pigskin, motioning for the ball, but Harrison shooed him away. That was not going to happen. This would be James Harrison's moment.

Townsend got the message, took off and blocked Warner, as Harrison swerved along the sidelines like an out-of-control rig, and a line of Steelers blockers formed. One by one, Harrison's teammates on the Steelers D cleared his path. Once Townsend

Members of the Harrison and Parise families gather in Tampa before Super Bowl XLIII.

knocked a back-peddling Warner out of the way, cornerback Ike Taylor hit someone trying to grab Harrison from behind. Hulking defensive end Brent Kiesel shoved another Cardinal off-stride as Harrison built momentum. Timmons laid a crack back block on another Arizona player. Fellow linebacker LaMarr Woodley then cut across Harrison's path to smack down two pursuers before tumbling in front of Harrison, threatening to do what none of the Cardinals could – bring Harrison down.

Dog-tired, Harrison still had enough left to jump over Woodley, when out of the corner of his eye he saw another red shirt. Fully aware that time had expired, he started high-stepping to avoid being downed by a diving Cardinal.

After safety Ryan Clark pushed away a few more defenders as he approached the goal line, the weary Harrison wrestled with the final two Cardinals who jumped him from behind, grabbing furiously at the ball as they rolled head-first in a tangled web of bodies into the end zone.

Touchdown! Pandemonium in Steeler Nation! A likely 14-point turn-around in a matter of seconds!

What had shaped up as a possible 14-10 halftime lead and a momentum-builder for the Cardinals had become what would prove to be (barely) an insurmountable 17-7 lead for the Steelers.

As the crowd roared, Harrison writhed in agony from landing on his head. He felt sharp pain shooting down his back from his neck as he lay in the end zone. Clark ran over to see why Harrison was still on the ground and found his teammate in need of help. "My neck! My neck!" were the only words that came out of Harrison's mouth.

He wasn't the only one hurting. In the enormous celebration in the stands, his mother Mildred was sandwiched between her husband and son. "When he finally makes it all the way, they go to grabbing and hugging, and I'm caught in the middle and hurt my back," she said.

On the other side of James Sr. was Harrison's chiropractor, who grabbed the player's dad and kissed him on the mouth, shocking him to the point where every time the elder Harrison turned to him again, he playfully covered his mouth.

In front of them, Harrison's agent Bill Parise and his wife Linda screamed, "We're going to Disney World," figuring Harrison was a lock for the trip as Super Bowl MVP.

But was the celebrating in vain? The only thing immediately certain was the game clock had expired. For several minutes, officials reviewed tape to determine whether the longest play in Super Bowl history ended with six points or if the hyper-ventilating linebacker had been downed a fraction of a yard short.

As the review went on, Harrison wearily regained his feet, moved to the bench and began an extensive encounter with an oxygen mask that would become fodder for a spoof on "Saturday Night Live" a week later. Up in the stands, his exhausted dad shouted: "Give me the oxygen. I'll go all the way with it."

From the bench, Harrison did not see game officials declare the play a touchdown. He didn't have to. A deafening roar from the black-and-gold-filled stadium told him he was the author of the longest play in Super Bowl history, a record that will never be surpassed. "Oh, I was positive I was in the end zone," he said. "There's no way I wasn't in."

LeBeau was thoroughly impressed with the linebacker's thought process. "He said he knew the time was getting short, they didn't have any timeouts, so they were not going to run the ball because the half would expire if they didn't get in," LeBeau said. "Figuring they were going to pass it, he dropped back and made a play," the coach gushed. The coach said that play was the turning point of the game, although the Steelers had to be bailed out in the last minute by Santonio Holmes' remarkable touchdown catch.

"As a coach, that is exactly what you want your players to do on the field. He was aware of the conditions, he went through that progression. When he told me that, I was as pleased as I could be that he didn't blitz on that play. What I am always looking for in players is for them to think and make smart plays, and that was a really smart play," said the coach, who has more than 50 years as an NFL player and coach and is known as the originator of the celebrated zone blitz defense.

LeBeau was not only elated with Harrison's effort but also the way his teammates escorted him down the field, clearing his way. "That's why as a coach, it doesn't ever get any better than that. I don't think we'll ever see a better play," he said.

While that play could not have been more remarkable, on the same field just a few hours later, the other side of Harrison emerged as it has so often in his life. The game would stand as a metaphor for Harrison's career – prodigious talent and hard-won success accompanied by often self-sabotaging behavior that would cripple the dreams of many.

With just 3:26 left in the game, the only league MVP in recent years playing on special teams because he is arguably the league's best wedge-buster was defending his lane on a punt return when a Cardinal reserve named Aaron Francisco tried to cut his knees with a block.

The street justice instilled by his mother in West Akron would come to the fore, a righteousness where there is no gray area. Everything is black and white, right or wrong.

He survived the tough Akron environment by living his mom's credo: When you're right, stand up for yourself. When you're wrong, don't mince words or lie about it; take your punishment and move on. It might have been a good way to rise above the troubled streets around him. It was also one that repeatedly derailed him, as it almost did on the NFL's biggest stage just a few hours after his biggest triumph.

Just as his mother had taught him, the 242-pound Harrison decided to exact justice on the spot. He angrily tossed Francisco to the ground, hovering over him with a flex of his hulking arms, as the downed Cardinal mouthed off, saying he had no class. Caught up in the moment, Harrison offered a salty response. Although he can't recall his exact words, "I can tell you this: It wasn't nice," he said.

As the play was coming to an end more than 30 yards away

from this one-sided melee, Francisco tried to regain his footing, but Harrison swatted him down again with an emasculating open palm. When the Cardinal tried to get up once more, Harrison gave him a two-handed shove back onto the ground, drawing an unnecessary roughness penalty that could have been a game-changer, even if it did not occur near the ball.

"I'm not trying to injure anybody, but I'm not opposed to hurting anyone on the football field if they try to do the same to me," a remorseless Harrison said about Francisco. "That's when I like hurting people."

After the game, Harrison approached Francisco to see if there was anything to finish. "I wanted to see what was up," he said. After bringing up Francisco's "no class" comment, the Cardinal said it was a product of the intensity of the game. While Harrison had no qualms about finishing things between them if Francisco so desired, he learned during the off season that the Cardinal who tormented him was a "real good dude." He said he talked to Francisco after the two teams met again to open the 2009 preseason and he was happy they were able to amicably resolve any issues between them.

Harrison wasn't very happy when he learned Fox analyst John Madden, the now-retired icon of the broadcast booth, provoked an army of Internet bloggers into racist rages and over-the-top rants – some from Steeler Nation – for suggesting he should have been tossed out of the game for the infraction.

Harrison characterizes his actions as just a bit overzealous, but, even months later, after discussing the play with a former Steeler who is now a Cardinal, he made no apologies.

"I have no concerns what people say about me. They talked about Jesus and he was a far better man than me so why wouldn't they talk about me?"

That play could have changed the outcome of the game, but it didn't. Aside from the Internet criticism and suggestions that the play might have cost him the Super Bowl MVP trophy that went to Holmes, it did not affect him or his team as other actions and reactions that have repeatedly undermined his success.

The reality is those wide-ranging ups and downs of Super Bowl XLIII are metaphors for the volatile roller coaster life of James Harrison. They reveal a man who overcame great odds to become the best defensive player in the league through a seldom seen power of will. While that focus has brought him fame and earned him millions, it also carries the baggage of a man who will react on a moment's notice when someone like Francisco affronts him.

Sometimes it's good. Sometimes it's bad. In James Harrison's life, there is no in-between. His hardscrabble parents taught him that the gray area is no place to be if you want to survive. From boyhood, they taught him to act tough, even if he wasn't. Create a psychological shield around you with a foreboding glare and a menacing demeanor to keep people away. Trust is earned, not given. If you look a man in the eye, you'd better be ready for whatever he has to bring. Most importantly, don't back down. Don't start anything. Finish things. The weak get destroyed.

That karmic essence has worked impeccably on the football field since he was a young kid, giving Harrison an edge that some say borders on the maniacal. To those who know him, it is also a shield he has used to cover up his extreme shyness. In the rest of his life, that edge has cut him repeatedly and profusely, forcing him to overcome daunting obstacles.

Whatever the outcome, he never looks back in life or in his beloved profession. Good or bad – and there is plenty of both – when things are over in Harrison's world, he lives with it. To dwell on the past is a prescription for future failure. In fact, while he has seen snippets of replays of his historic Super Bowl effort, he has never sat down alone and watched the whole thing.

His agent and friend Parise says Harrison is like no one he has ever met. "Life is very simple to James," he said. "Do the right thing, do it the best you can, and you take whatever consequences are out there. To James, life is simple. We make it hard."

2

Growing up Harrison

James Harrison was among the exceptions in West Akron. He grew in a two-parent household, and his parents took extreme measures to instill their fundamental credo that life was hard, and you had to be tough to survive. No one knew that better than his strict, iron-willed mother Mildred.

A high school dropout who married at 16, Mildred had five young children before she turned 20. Her brood would grow to six children, even as her marriage fell apart. For a time she was on her own, scratching out a living with only a brother with a good-paying job at a nearby Chrysler plant to help her support the kids until she met the man who would become her second husband at age 24.

Eventually, she fell for James Harrison, a former baseball star who made it to the Class AA professional ranks before entering the U.S. Army and starring in softball and boxing. He moved to Akron from Maryland after his own failed marriage. By the time they married, the couple had 13 kids between them and moved to a dead end called Minerva Street on Akron's tough West Side.

Incredibly, in one horrific stroke, the family grew by another eight children when Mildred's sister was murdered and the Harrisons took them in. So by the time James Harrison Jr. was born, he had 21 siblings, although the closest in age was eight years older.

With all of those children, and the children's children soon to come, the Harrisons moved from Minerva to Noah Avenue, a large, blue three-story dwelling that Mildred says "was the biggest house I could afford."

While many of the children had grown and left home by the time James Jr. was born, for as long as he remembers, there were kids all over the place – some his age, some not, some brothers and sisters, some cousins and some the kids of all of the above, which made for a confusing upbringing.

"I have a grandson who is one year older than James," Mildred says. So bewildering was this large brood that James Jr. didn't realize one of the older kids was his blood brother until he was a teenager.

One thing that came with living in the Harrison household was discipline, which almost miraculously allowed all of them to be raised in a low-income, poverty-riddled neighborhood without falling victim to crime, prison or drug addiction like so many of their peers. "I think my kids came through because of me. I was very stern, believed in discipline," Mildred said as the assembled children, even though now adults, nodded nervously in agreement in an interview.

One example of her discipline came many years later when she received an unsolicited handwritten letter from Harrison's fifth grade teacher, Mrs. Hall. The teacher said she'd read about the son's great success in the NFL. She said since James had a penchant for letting his mind wander, she sat him right in front of her desk with hopes of keeping his attention "as I knew he could

James Harrison's kindergarten photo.

do all that was asked of him if he wanted to do it," read the letter that Mildred still keeps in a scrapbook. "You always told me if he wouldn't do what he was supposed to do to just call and you'd be right up to school."

That happened twice and, according to Mrs. Hall's letter, "when he came back he was very cooperative and did all his work. I would like to praise you for always taking the time for James."

Education was the key. The high school dropout insisted that all of her children get diplomas. In fact, she was so determined to set an example that she earned her own General Equivalency Diploma years after she quit school to have babies. "I can't insist they give me one if I don't have one, so I went back and got it," she says proudly of the certificate she received in 1993.

The discipline covered all aspects of life. It included not only a close eye on everything going on, but also reliance on the children to tell their mother immediately if something was awry. And they'd better not lie. To this day, James Jr. is incapable of even a mild prevarication – another of his mother-instilled traits that sometimes has had negative consequences.

"You couldn't walk out the door before they'd tell mama what their brother was doing," she laughs. In reality, they all knew the price that would be paid if they didn't tell their mother. She admits she did not spare the rod. She also would catch them doing wrong by eavesdropping on phone conversations or checking their rooms.

"They say don't spy on children. Well, my thing was, that's not your room. It's my room. You are living in my room. You do what I say," she says with a raised voice. "Even my older kids would respect me and my house, and to this day, you must respect my house."

While both parents were well-schooled in raising children by the time baby James came along on May 4, 1978, they were frustrated early on about how to control this rambunctious young "mama's boy."

While he was shy, the youngest child exhibited extraordinary

James Harrison plays in the snow in W. Akron

strength from infancy. When he was just a toddler, his father had trouble keeping him out of the street. So he tied one end of a rope around his waist, the other to a porch rail.

The outcome was not only a severely weakened porch rail, but the first displays of the fierce, insatiable will his son exhibits to this day. Young James would get even with the kids who taunted him as if he were an angry pit bull on a leash. Some of them who came close would feel his wrath just as the Cardinals' Aaron Francisco and other NFL players who entered the powerful linebacker's domain have.

Those kids on Noah Avenue would learn that if you mess with

James Harrison, there would be a price to pay. In fact, "Pit Bull" was one of his first nicknames. It didn't stem from his dad's rope trick or James' affection for that breed that would surface later, but because one of his aunts said he resembled the wide-necked dog. That confrontational approach was born of a tough life lesson from his mother: Face your fears head on.

One time David Walker, a friend who lived across the street, tried to intimidate James with faux karate kicks, which convinced his mother that James Jr. was afraid of the smaller kid. So she sent him out to settle things once and for all. "I'll bet I can hit harder than him," said his mom, suggesting what would happen if her youngest child didn't face his fears. "I wasn't scared of him, but I went out there, and we ended up getting it up one day," James said of the ensuing tussle he can now laugh at. He and Walker remain friends.

As he grew up, the tougher-by-the-day West Akron streets were no place for kids after dark, and his mother made sure all of them knew it. "We had a street-light rule," James said. "When the light in front of the house came on, you'd better have yourself in the house, or there was a price to pay."

His mom's words were law, and if any of the Harrison kids wanted to sass their parents, his mother's response was simple: "If they wanted to talk, then I'd give them something to talk about," she said with a twinkle in her eyes, without having to elaborate. "They didn't want to play with me."

The neighborhood would rapidly deteriorate over James' childhood, and in the early 1990s, street gangs were entrenched in Akron, as in most every other inner city in America. Harrison says the gang violence was nothing like what goes on in large American cities, but he remembers that one kid was murdered over gang affiliations before he got to high school. He knew gangs but never joined.

"I got 13 brothers and sisters, so I felt that I really didn't need that," he said. Besides, his father's admonition stayed with him: "My dad told me only punks and pussies join gangs. I didn't feel

A smiling Harrison in his school
photo from fifth grade.

like I was either one of them, so I didn't join."

The worst that happened to him was feeling pressure from an occasional bully. When one street tough became threatening, he took a stand right out of the Mildred Harrison playbook: "I tried to hit him in the head with a brick. I didn't have any problems again," he deadpans. "If somebody messes with you, you defend yourself. You don't go out and look for trouble, but if trouble comes to you, you don't run..." he said. That childhood mantra is one he still uses on the football field.

But Mildred's black-and-white guide to street survival did not always fit in with school disciplinary rules, which to her dismay did not tolerate fighting. "All that does is carry it on outside the school, where things can get worse. I told James and all my kids if somebody picks on them, I expected them to do what they have to do. That's how you deal with it," is the way his mother's street doctrine goes.

At the time, James Jr. was already fairly stocky, but he acknowledges he got a pass from some confrontations because everyone in the neighborhood knew he had lots of brothers and sisters who had his back. Not that there wasn't the occasional scrape. When he was 16, a neighbor sprayed him with a high-powered squirt gun. Harrison beat the 23-year-old man so badly that he cracked a knuckle on his own right hand.

Parise, the agent who has become a close friend of the Harrison family over the past six years, says James's parents "doted over him and protected him. She was a woman who was beaten down by white people all her life, so she doesn't trust too many people. I enjoy her great wisdom, which is street taught. Some of it might be a little misguided in my world or your world, but not in her world."

Mildred admits she has almost no trust for folks outside the family. It was something earned, not given. In fact, she spent most of her life building a mistrust of people because of the way they treated her. For better or worse, she ingrained that in her youngest child, something he carries with him to this day. "To be honest, I blindly trust nobody. I trust certain people to an extent, but I don't blindly trust anybody," he said.

Even today, Harrison puts up an impenetrable shield of emotional protection that allows for little talk or show of feelings, unless someone affronts him. To show feelings is to show weakness, his mother taught him, and only the strong survive. Those he does bring into his domain – which is a short list outside his family – find a bright, engaging man not opposed to practical jokes or lively banter, whether it be during a workout, at his home or in the locker room. The folks he trusts also find a man willing to go out of his way to help them.

Eye contact – or lack of it – was another issue that many years later would cause some NFL types to say it made him appear

David Walker, Harrison's best friend growing up, and James
Harrison after they suited up for a big game in Pee Wee
football.

aloof or even stupid. The way he was brought up, folks did not stare each other down unless they were itching for a fight. Ironically, it was Harrison who won a playful "stare-down" with then Steelers cornerback Bryant McFadden in the locker room during Super Bowl week. "How did I win? I didn't blink my eyes," he recalled jokingly.

"I mean, eye contact, it's not that big a deal. Right now, these little crazy kids on the streets are starting stuff because someone looks at them wrong. How the hell do you look at somebody wrong? What can somebody do to you without physically touching you that could make you want to kill them. I mean, have they all done lost their minds?" he says peering directly into his interviewer's eyes.

A focused work ethic was also instilled in the Harrison children. "James always worked," his mother said. "He always had things to do, chores, work. I think that was real important, part of how he was shaped and how he grew." For James, who has worked at a nursing home and driven a bus for awhile in college, one of his first formal jobs was helping out at Portage Broom and Brush, a cleaning chemical business where his dad worked. It led to Harrison learning to drive at a young age.

Before he reached the age of 10, his father let him fool around driving cars in the family's driveway, while sitting on his dad's lap. Harrison's first solo memory behind the wheel involved his dad's Ford Escort, which is just a tad bigger than the Smart Car Harrison made a splash with at the 2009 Steelers training camp. The Escort had a manual transmission, which James had never operated. His first move, unfortunately, was to crank it into reverse, bolting the car backward before it came to a sudden stop just short of a neighbor's wall.

In the ensuing years, his father – who delivered chemicals all over Ohio – would take James Jr. to work with him in the summer, eventually putting him behind the wheel of his van so he could sneak in a nap between stops. James was 12 and, of course, unlicensed, but he learned the roads of Ohio.

A teenaged James Harrison flexes his muscles in his sister's back yard in Akron.

Not that everything went smoothly. One day James Jr. was cruising on a two-lane highway when a big rig approached from the other direction. "I got nervous so I veered away from the truck near a ditch on the side of the road," the younger Harrison laughs. That woke up Dad, who grabbed the wheel, straightened it out and said, "Be careful" before going right back to sleep. That wasn't the only time he showed confidence in his son's precocious driving.

Once, his dad woke up to find James cruising at 75 miles per hour. "He told me I shouldn't be speeding," the son said, "so I told him I was following the flow of traffic just like he said." James Sr., by no means the disciplinarian his wife was, simply nodded and dozed off again.

James Sr. with Sweet Baby James.

3

Mama Don't Want
Her Baby to Grow Up
To Play Football

It was clear early on that James Harrison, although he wasn't that big, was a very strong boy. But while his mother let him participate in a wrestling program, she regularly balked at letting her youngest child do anything she considered a threat to his health. Quite simply, she was afraid he'd get hurt.

So it took some doing to get her to allow him to join a program that would change the course of his life. She didn't mind him playing ball in the yard, but she didn't want him in organized football. "I'd tell everyone, 'Look at this precious little baby.' I couldn't have people beating on him," she said. Fortunately for the Pittsburgh Steelers, though it took weeks, young James and David Walker, who remains his best friend, eventually cajoled his mother into letting him play Pee Wee football.

The first practice was almost his last. After a lengthy workout that included lots of running, he woke up the next day with intense muscle pain. When Walker came to get him for the second day of practice, he balked at going back.

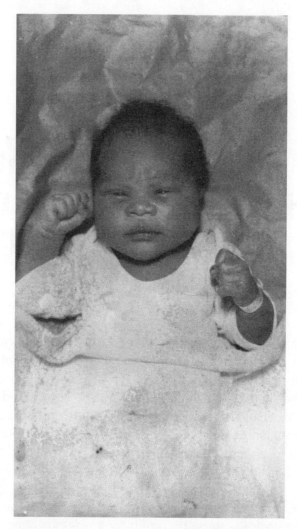

James Harrison on May 4, 1978, the day he was born.

"My body hurt, I couldn't breathe and I felt like I was sucking air through a straw. I swear I had an asthma attack," Harrison said. He went to the doctor. "You don't have asthma," was the verdict. So it was back to football for James.

James Sr. remembers other rough spots. His job kept him from attending all of his son's practices. When he was there, he started to see his son displaying the same kind of intense, reckless abandon that typifies his playing style in the NFL. "He was like a pit bull, so aggressive on the field," the father said. That's why James Sr. was unnerved when his child told him a coach wanted to cut him from the team. To the frustrated coach, James seemed distant, wouldn't listen and appeared lazy when they ran laps and other drills – but not all the time. "The coach told me 'when you're not here, James doesn't do'," James Sr. said.

So the father told his son, "You are either going to play hard all the time or give it up." End of discussion. The son said he wanted to play, even if he didn't like to run. As time went on, other coaches would raise the same issues over the stellar athlete's way of initially relating to them, of not quite getting with the program.

The Harrison shield, not letting outsiders into his world until he built some hard-earned trust in them, would emerge. It threatened to abruptly end his dream in little league football, in high school, college and the pros, where he was cut repeatedly before he became a star.

Once the youngest Harrison focused on playing all-out every time he stepped onto the field as a pre-teen, the world began to open up to him. And while his family wasn't exactly flush with money, they were better off than many. "Growing up, I didn't always get what I wanted, but I did get what I needed," he said. His parents used their meager earnings from several jobs to keep the huge family afloat. When he started playing, his mother decided the team-issued helmets were less than safe, so she scrounged enough money to buy him his own headgear and other equipment. "Their equipment was terrible," she said.

"I could see him getting a concussion because he was flying all over the place. We needed to protect him."

He quickly became a standout Pee Wee player, playing on both sides of the ball. While most kids harbor delusions of grandeur, Harrison did not. Yes, he was a Cleveland Browns fan, like most kids in Northeastern Ohio in the early 1990s. He was particularly fond of quarterback Bernie Kosar. He loved watching the quickness and grace of scat back Eric Metcalf and kept close tabs on running back Kevin Mack and receiver Webster Slaughter. But he says he never entertained thoughts of becoming a professional football player. He also followed Indians slugger Albert Belle, the iconoclastic outfielder, but neither then or now did he look at sports figures as heroes or aspire to be like them. In fact, to this day, he rarely even watches sporting events on television, including reruns of his own performances.

Harrison has met fellow Akronite and Cleveland Cavaliers star LeBron James, but they are not close. "I have a hard time understanding why someone would look up to an athlete or an actor or whatever they may be, and aspire to be like them. My heroes were in the house ... mom and dad!" he said.

With his mother's prodding, after he was held back in first grade, Harrison built above-average grades during his eight years in the Akron public school system in a building where 94 percent of the students were black, 90 percent classified as "economically disadvantaged."

Because he was held back in first grade, and since Akron's public schools did not have a junior high football program, Harrison was too old to play Pee Wee football in eighth grade, a year in which his body grew into the beginnings of the sculpted man he would become.

Despite the missing year, decent grades and his growing football credentials prompted the family to think beyond West Akron. His dad's boss helped James get into Catholic, predominately white Archbishop Hoban High School, across town from nearly all-black Buchtel High School just a few blocks away from home.

It would prove to be a disaster.

4

Into the Great White WAY?

While the family was not Catholic, James Sr.'s boss thought the parochial school would allow the younger Harrison to excel as a student athlete, even if it meant crossing his first cultural bridge.

Mom was all for it. While she didn't often see gang activity on the streets of West Akron, she knew it was present and knew the deplorable state of the Akron schools. "I thought this might be better for him, that he would get a better education at Hoban," she recalled.

It would be the first time James Jr. would venture away from his close-knit family and neighborhood. It was a cultural shock all right, and it wasn't only about race.

"I was in public schools all the way up, and I saw drugs one time," he recalled. "When I got to Hoban, I saw more drugs there than I had seen in my whole life. Acid, pills, weed, coke, you name it,"

Hoban's coach was the legendary Maurice "Mo" Tipton, who

Mildred Harrison hugs her tuxedo-clad son as he prepared for his sixth grade commencement.

James Sr. and James Jr. as he was suited in a white
tuxedo for his sixth grade graduation.

had built his reputation coaching in Orrville, Ohio, the home of
Smucker's jelly. After his retirement there, he took the Hoban
job with the hope that he could use open enrollment policies to
build a football powerhouse in Akron, his hometown and about
an hour's drive north from where he lived.

He still remembers his initial encounters with Harrison that
mirror what his Pee Wee coach found. "He was very quiet, sort of
standoffish, so I kind of let him go. He'd stand on the sidelines
and watch what we were doing. He wouldn't try anything unless
he knew what was going on, but once he did, he became more
and more involved," he said.

While Tipton had coached several players who achieved great

Harrison wasn't always as big as he is today, but while he was a shy child, he never ran away from a chance to flex his "pipes" for a camera.

things at major universities and in the pros, what he found in Harrison was something he still considers special.

"His freshman year, he showed us this natural snap to his body, where he could come out of a stance and bam, hit someone with tremendous force. It was just a natural thing," Tipton said.

Soon after his arrival, it was clear no one could handle the powerful Harrison.

"I still remember I put him one-on-one with a senior tight end when he was a freshman and he couldn't handle James. We were so impressed. Obviously he was going to be a good player, but that particular play in practice stuck in my mind," he said. On the field then, as now, Harrison said he was not intimidated by a guy three years older than him.

While he had some adjustment difficulties, Harrison performed so well as a freshman that the coaches wanted to promote him to the varsity before the end of the season. But his mother balked, fearful once again that her baby would get hurt.

That would turn out to be an unwarranted fear. His career at the Catholic school would come to an abrupt end in his first semester, and it happened because he followed his mother's long-standing admonition: Never start anything, but never back down.

A 12th grader accused Harrison of stealing an address book filled with juicy details of the senior's extracurricular activities with women and drugs. Actually, one of Harrison's friends had the book, but James was not about to rat out his buddy.

Eventually, the senior and some of his friends accosted Harrison in a hallway. The confrontation ended quickly with a one-punch knockout, the senior in the hospital and Harrison whisked off to the principal's office and immediately suspended. He clearly did not realize his own power.

"He was acting all hard, and as soon as I got close to him, I punched him in his face, and he went out cold," said Harrison, who considers himself the victim in the incident. While that was not his first school fight or the last, Harrison refused to apologize because the other guy started it. And so there was a quick transfer back to his neighborhood school.

"They wanted me to kiss their ass to stay. That's not going to happen," he said, offering no regrets almost 20 years later. "I wasn't sorry for it then. I'm still not sorry for it."

Like Francisco in the Super Bowl, the senior at Hoban had to pay because he violated the Harrison sense of right and wrong, even if he was the one who paid dearly for it. It would not be the last time he would be punished for his convictions.

While Tipton said the Brothers of the Holy Cross at Hoban treated him well during his brief stint there, he did not like what they did to Harrison. "I didn't think he was getting a fair shake. It might have been because the kid he hit was part of a family that was well-connected to the school. I was upset. There is no question about it because they made a real fast call and didn't even contact me. He was out before I even knew it."

So when the coaching job at Coventry High School, south of Akron in the Portage Lakes area, opened up, Tipton and his staff made the move. And so did Harrison.

Using Ohio's open enrollment policies, which allow students to transfer without losing athletic eligibility, James transferred, becoming one of a handful of minority students at Coventry. Although just 10 miles from West Akron, the lily-white school might as well have been another planet to Harrison. He learned of the racial divide before he ever attended a class.

"The principal told us he would probably hear them using the 'N-word,'" his mother recalled. "He said there was a bunch of ignorant red necks – excuse my language – and that is just the way it is," said James.

The principal knew of Harrison's retaliatory actions at Hoban, and the coaches had mentioned his distant and sometimes surly demeanor – especially if someone started something. So he implored James to come to him if something untoward happened. While his mother always schooled him to finish what others started, the new principal asked James to walk away from trouble, a trait foreign to his psyche.

Racism would find him from the start. There was the time he choked a kid who called him "nigger" under his breath, and another time he beat up a pickup-truckload of race-baiting, pipe-wielding Coventry graduates. He had a few other run-ins, but nothing that got him into major trouble.

For most of his high school career, he maintained a low "B" average, while excelling on the football team and as a track athlete. He would lead the Coventry Comets to an unprecedented 25-5 record over three years. The school hasn't reached those heights since. A tailback, he rushed for more than 1,000 yards two years in a row, averaging 12 yards a carry his senior year. He led his team in tackles, earned all-conference accolades and emerged as a potential recruit worthy of consideration from major colleges such as Ohio State, Notre Dame, Oklahoma State and Nebraska.

His dad said he always believed James could have been an outstanding running back in college but for one thing: "He didn't want to run around people. His thing was to run over them. He'd be in the open with one man left. All he had to do is fake him out and go in. He'd fake him all right, but then go right into him. At that age, a lot of kids don't want to do that."

Mildred Harrison remembers just before his senior year, Tipton told her what his coaching staff had been discussing for a year or so—that James was good enough to play on Sundays. "I had not thought about it," James says. "My goal was to play high school ball, and then I got a chance to play in college, but I never really thought that far down the road (pro football)."

After his junior year, college football was definitely on the horizon. Harrison was so highly regarded he could have pretty much gone wherever he wanted. Then, like an omen for the future, the bottom began to drop out. After a year of acclaim leading up to his senior season, Harrison admits he did not perform well in a preseason scrimmage. "I actually stood and watched as two of my teammates got dragged into the end zone. It was like an out-of-body experience where I was watching myself watch this happen," he said.

After the scrimmage, one of his teammates told Harrison a coach was hollering about his play outside the bus, saying, "This guy's supposed to be an all-star and he ain't shit."

So Harrison set out to confront him. He wrestled with a teammate and another coach trying to prevent him from getting to the coach who had been bad-mouthing him.

"He should have manned up and backed up what he said," Harrison said. If he had, Harrison said he probably would have accepted the criticism. What made him angry was that the put-down came behind his back.

The confrontation caused Tipton to suspend Harrison for the first two games of the season, which didn't help his reputation with recruiters, who already had heard about the Hoban incident.

While he was not allowed to play, Tipton was impressed when he saw his star player sitting with his parents in the front row, still supporting his teammates.

He returned with a vengeance after the suspension, tearing up competition through the season before he encountered more blatant racism he could not walk away from.

Playing mostly all-white competition from rural Ohio, he endured racial taunting from opposition fans because Coventry often won by large margins. Invariably, the abuse came from people cloaked in the anonymity of the crowd.

"You'd hear somebody holler a racial slur here and there, but it got to the point that you didn't care because we were beating everybody anyway," he said. "Most of the time, it was from people in the stands I couldn't get to, or somebody on the sidelines. The guys who were out on the field didn't say anything because they were out there where I could get to them."

The racist epithets were particularly galling in a late season game against Tuscarawas Valley, a mostly white school an hour south of Akron. While he constantly heard racist taunts, they became more pronounced after he made a series of defensive plays that influenced the game's outcome.

He got his second suspension – for his final game in high school – after receiving a penalty for celebrating a play in which he viciously tackled the quarterback. As he walked off the field, a chorus of racist abuse rained down on him, with someone from the crowd screaming, "Yeah, nigger, that's what you get." That's when Harrison made a vulgar gesture toward the stands, garnering a second personal foul and an automatic one-game-suspension. His team lost the league championship without him the next week.

He still ground out 1,000 yards rushing for the second consecutive time and led his team in defensive plays despite playing only seven games. After that suspension, more college coaches backed away. "They said, 'We can't take a chance if you are going to be a disciplinary problem, or you may or may not be around.' " he said, once again acknowledging that his own actions caused a detour in his life.

Despite his problems, Tipton, who posted a 198-73-6 career record and sent players to major colleges and the pros, says Harrison was not a bad guy as many thought and was one of the best players he ever coached.

Tipton reached back to a critical game late in Harrison's senior year when he opened with a belly option play that featured Harrison, a fullback, running off tackle. It worked so well, he did it again and again and again, calling the exact play about a dozen times in a row because the opposition couldn't stop Harrison. "I told him to hit the hole and cut back and make them tackle him. They couldn't."

One off-the-field transgression – at least in his mother's eyes – occurred when his brother Ross was home from the military on leave and took his little brother to get his first tattoo, a bold-faced "Harrison" around his right arm. His mother was initially outraged, but softened over the years when Harrison had one with praying hands in tribute to his beloved grandmother put on his left arm, and one that said "Mom and Dad" over his heart. His final piece of ink is the inscription "Colossians 1:16" from the Bible which says, "For by him all things were created, both in the heavens and on earth, visible and invisible – whether thrones or dominions or rulers or authorities – all things have been created through Him and for Him."

But events that embroiled Harrison as a senior were beginning to build his reputation as anything but a humble servant of the Lord. His various tribulations were earning him a reputation as a thug. While nothing could be further from the truth, Harrison did little then (as now) to dispel the notion that he is unapproachable, downright scary even.

Once again, the Harrison code, grounded in the mean streets of West Akron, would prove to be a major stumbling block, this time sealing his fate in the college-recruiting process.

James Harrison poses in his high school uniform.

5

Crimes of Coventry: "BB - Gate"

If the second suspension wasn't enough to chase away recruiters, an incident that simmered and boiled over in his senior year was. During preseason summer camp, a friend of Harrison brought a spring-loaded BB-pistol to practice for some good-natured locker room battles. They took turns chasing each other, launching stinging butt- and body-shots that caused no real injuries or produced any complaints.

Leon D. Hartman, Harrison's position coach working his first job after playing football at Kent State, heard about the prank and eventually caught Harrison shooting at a teammate. The coach grabbed the BB gun and in one motion shot a round at a player as a joke. Then he confiscated the gun and ordered everyone involved – himself included for shooting also – to do extra drills and running as punishment. He and the players thought was the end of it.

But it wasn't. And that had more to do with some disgruntled parents than with Harrison or Hartman. While they won an unprecedented number of games the previous two seasons, Tipton and his staff were under criticism because starters who grew up in Coventry were being displaced by Harrison and other players they brought in.

In Harrison's case, the abuse was particularly heavy with racist undertones. Leading the charge were the parents of a one-time Pee Wee star who was not a starter. He was not very fast and was no more than 5-foot-8 inches tall and 150 pounds, limiting his effectiveness in the rigors of Ohio high school football.

Tipton characterized the player as a "great kid" who realized he would get on the field only when the team was winning by large margins. Nonetheless, his dad, an athletic club leader, called a preseason meeting with the coach. Tipton remembers the dad excitedly describing his son's prospects for the next year when Coventry – with Harrison set to graduate but several new players coming in from other districts – was expected to be a major prep power.

Tipton thought the right thing to do was to break the news right away that his son probably would continue to be the backup running back. "I thought it would work better if they knew in advance," he said.

It didn't – for that man or the parents of others who could not bear to watch their sons standing on the sidelines while outsiders like James Harrison brought a team that never had a winning record to the brink of championships.

Hartman, like Tipton, also had several heated exchanges with parents, including the booster club leader's wife. "She'd come up to me and say, 'Why is this nigger playing in front of my son? He was the best player in Coventry history in grade school,'" Hartman recalled. "I told her the reason your son isn't playing is because he's not good enough."

Those parents and a few others were so upset that they sought to transfer their kids from Coventry to arch-rival Manchester just down the road. That's when the BB gun incident escalated into a political/legal drama that would change the lives of Harrison and Hartman.

The coaches had considered the event nothing more than a prank best handled internally, but that was not to be. "It be-

The Harrisons and their youngest child, the star of the Coventry Comets.

Harrison was also a stellar track athlete at Coventry High.

While his final year of high school was marred by scandal, James and Mildred celebrated his graduation.

came clear to me they wanted the black kid's head," said Hartman, who is white and was a teacher as well as a coach. "They blatantly told me, 'Turn the kid in and we'll keep it off you and sweep it under the rug.' "

"I told them this kid didn't really do anything wrong. This kid is going to play on Sundays, and you want to kick him out of school for nothing?"

Nonetheless, the booster club leader's wife, who had heard rumors for months about the incident, provoked an investigation. It eventually came into the hands of the Summit County Sheriff's Department. There were leaks from the disgruntled parents that ended up in the Akron Beacon Journal and on television news that turned what would be called "BB-Gate" into a full-scale probe with allegations of a coverup by school officials.

While several players were involved in the shootings, more and more pressure was applied to Harrison and Hartman, who was repeatedly offered a pass if he gave up Harrison. "I kept telling them I'm not rolling on this kid for something stupid," he said.

Harrison felt the same way. He admitted shooting a kid in the rear end with the BB gun but was not going to tell on anyone else. Eventually, he and others were persuaded to admit what they did, as well as the coach's action. Harrison is still pained today by what happened to the coach.

More than six months after the childish incident – in the middle of the crucial college recruiting period – Akron authorities filed assault-related charges against Harrison and Hartman. Hartman was also accused of trying to cajole students and officials into covering it up.

While virtually no one at the school – students, teachers, staff – made a big deal out of it, and many of them signed a petition supporting Harrison and Hartman, the parent who pushed the case remained steadfast in wanting Harrison removed from the school and the coach fired.

"I told James to basically lay low," Hartman said. "Don't say anything, but if you do, don't lie. If this didn't go away, I told him I'd let them turn it on me so he could ride it out, but the bottom line was they were out headhunting, looking for a lynching. I had parents come up to me and say they were going to get me out of the school and all of the blacks that came with you," he said.

Aside from the notion that Harrison's play caused their children to be benched, he said, his stone-faced demeanor – the shield – provoked fear among Coventry's white students. They did not like the fact that he dated a white student either. "They wanted him to go down, wanted him out of the school. They were all scared of him," said Hartman, adding that Harrison was never malicious toward him or anyone else.

"They can say whatever they want, but it was purely racial. Don't even think it wasn't. He was the only brother on the team, and we were planning on bringing in three more the next year. They knew (the white kids) would not play," Hartman said.

Harrison looks back on the whole episode with astonishment. "They made it out like I was trying to assassinate someone. It was actually a big joke that hurt no one," he said.

In fact, when the sheriff's investigators took Harrison to headquarters, he immediately confessed to shooting at one kid. "I told the detective I shot the one dude, but he thought I was lying," he said. They made it sound like he was a serial shooter out to maim everyone in his path.

The cop tried unsuccessfully to intimidate him. "He said 'You think you are going to sit here and say nothing? I've broke murderers and killers, and I'm going to break you too.' But I told him I haven't killed anybody," Harrison says of that mystifying period. "They said they were going to charge me because I was 18, but what it came down to was, I was the only black."

Both eventually pleaded to reduced charges and paid fines. But they paid a heavier price. Hartman lost his teacher's license. Harrison's once seemingly bright path to a college football career was all but extinguished.

"I did something wrong, and I was ashamed of it," Hartman

said. "I know it wasn't malicious, but it was wrong." He took a job in a mill near Warren, Ohio, where he still works, but eventually was able to reclaim his teacher's license. He never went back into the classroom but is now a high school coach, runs a successful youth football program and has been elected to his area's school board where he won 75 percent of the vote. He has never hidden his past because he believes it was an absurd overreaction by people with bad intentions.

He still regrets his own actions with the BB gun but not his actions in the aftermath related to Harrison. "Teaching is a great career, but I learned there are other things that are more important, and that kid was one of them for me," he said. Considering whether the series of events amounted to an injustice, Hartman scoffed. "There is justice in the world. James Harrison is playing on Sundays. That was the justice for me. They were trying to ruin a kid, and I wasn't going to let it happen, and I'd do the same thing again."

The parent who pushed the case could not be found for an interview, but her lawyer, Allen Schulman of Canton, said it was Hartman who forced her hand. "She clearly was not out to ruin James Harrison, but was simply outraged by what she perceived was a coverup by school officials and coaches," he said. The woman said her son's physical education class grades were lowered over her actions against the coach and player.

Harrison dismisses the claim: "They can say what they want, but I was the only player to go down when several others did the same thing."

For Tipton, Hartman and the rest of the Coventry football staff that had quickly turned a perennial loser into a winner, the events surrounding the BB gun incident and the way Harrison was treated were too much.

In his letter of resignation that ended his storied career, Tipton said it was time to "take a stand" against "a small, disgruntled and racist faction within the community, who wish to control coaching staff's decisions by undermining the staff and adminis-

James Harrison celebrates with his mother after signing
a letter of intent to attend Kent State University after every
other school spurned him over high school tribulations.

tration at Coventry High School. This group, motivated by self-interest and who hold their own personal vendettas above the betterment and continued success of the school and the football program, have made coaching football at Coventry unbearable. Some of these parents seem to have a problem with players who are minorities. We're coaches. We don't recognize race on the field. We recognize skill."

But would any other football coach recognize James Harrison's skill?

6

Where Have All the Recruiters Gone?

When Harrison finally went to court, the judge voiced exasperation that the case had even gotten that far. He reduced the charges to a disorderly conduct count and fined Harrison $100.

By that time, the college recruiters were long gone. They refused to take a chance on a kid they believed could not get along with coaches or teammates or even fans.

The word "thug" seemed permanently attached to his name. Harrison admits his stone-faced demeanor instilled by his mother may have contributed to his image. But, in fact, all of his coaches from that era to this day voice genuine affection for Harrison.

His scholarship chances were further doomed because he let his grades slip during the legal mess. While he had a low "B" average in school, after five tries, he came up one point short on the standardized ACT college entrance exam, making him ineligible under NCAA rules known as Proposition 48 to play football as a college freshman.

Harrison is still frustrated by his failure on the standardized test. "I just could not get it," he said of that one point. There

Some of the Harrisons get ready for a ride to watch James play for
Kent State.

were no scholarship offers left.

Those problems would be enough for most individuals to give up on the dream of a college education and football career. Not Harrison. "I didn't really dwell on that. Nothing I could do about it. Even if it was something I did to put myself in that situation, all I could do is move forward," he said. "Weak people worry about things that are over.

"Everything happens for a reason, good, bad or indifferent. Right now, I'm happy where it ended. If it wasn't for that, I may have taken another ride, gone to a big school. Who knows what would have happened with coaches and so on and so forth."

The only shot at a scholarship came from Kent State, not exactly an elite football program, and even at that the coaching staff was divided over whether they wanted a guy like Harrison on their roster. In 1995, coach James Corrigall was beginning a two-year stint trying to revive the long-losing program there. He became interested when Todd Murgatroyd, a linebacker coach, brought in the impressive tape of Harrison's high school games.

"I figured he could help us offensively and defensively. I mean, I was thinking he could play both ways," said Corrigall, now an assistant coach at Hiram College. So he asked Murgatroyd to set up a meeting with Harrison. "When I looked at him and looked in his eyes, I knew there was something inside this kid," he said.

Corrigall, who played at Kent and afterwards a dozen years in the Canadian Football League, said he knew all about Harrison's issues with coaches and the criminal matter, as well as the negative perception about the kid from West Akron. "I expected to see a guy who dressed like one, acted like one, but his persona never exhibited thuggery," Corrigall said. "He was very quiet, very unassuming, a very 'yes, sir, no sir' type of a guy. It's the old thing: Never judge a book by its cover."

He decided to take a chance on Harrison because of advice his priest gave him when he was young. "Always give a kid another chance, and if he shits on you, give him another chance, and if he shits on you, give him another chance," he said.

"I was that kid they had given another chance to because I had been in severe difficulties, and they had always given me another chance and resurrected me. I saw what had happened in my life because a priest took two or three chances with me."

He was further sold when he met the family. "I knew he had a good set of parents. There was good stock in this kid, and it was just a matter of time when this was going to come to the fore-front. Now, when it was going to come to the forefront I had no idea," he said.

Corrigall related to Harrison because "we were both kind of nuts from the point of view that we both went off and did very immature things without thinking about what we were doing, and there were people that were trying to push us off the shelf and get rid of us. But there were other people trying to revive us and help us because they saw something in us that nobody else did. I decided this is a guy we are going to pursue because I saw good in him; I didn't care about the BB gun. I didn't care that he reared up and got nasty with a coach. I can handle that. I saw in his eyes he was sincere. This guy's no dummy."

While some of his assistants were against the pursuit of Harri-son, and athletic administrators cast a wary eye, Kent State gave Harrison his only NCAA Division I offer. The plan was to enroll on his parents' dime and receive a scholarship once he gained eligi-bility the following year. "Usually I measure people with my gut. I just felt this kid deserved a chance," Corrigall said.

He would never get to see Harrison rise to stardom because he was fired before Harrison became eligible. But he would keep tabs on Harrison's performances. "Every time I heard something good about James, I'd say, "Goddammit, that guy is going to be OK,' " he gushed.

Murgatroyd was retained by new coach Dean Pees, now the defensive coordinator for the New England Patriots. He became Harrison's handler and position coach for two years.

Because Harrison was a Proposition 48 non-qualifier, the coach-ing staff had very little contact with him for over a year until he finally regained his eligibility. "It was up to James to sink or swim," Murgatroyd said.

The Harrisons had little money, but they did not want to thwart their son's dream of playing college football, so they scraped together the funds to send their last child to Kent State. "He told me he wanted to play football and develop himself. I wasn't going to be the one who cut my son short," said his dad. "I told him it was going to be OK. He'd fight through this."

Said James Jr.: "I was just going to go wherever I could get a chance."

Harrison's ferocious play in college caused numerous
newspaper stories like this one in the Akron Beacon
Journal featuring his reckless style at Kent State.

7

Bust Not Boom
At Kent State

Harrison says he had a great time in his first year at Kent, but it had almost nothing to do with anything approximating formal education. He spent his time smoking, drinking and partying, failing all but one of his courses the first semester. He still had not become eligible for football, and his mother had had enough.

She had already issued an ultimatum to hit the books or come home and go to work by the time his second semester grade report arrived showing no improvement:

"I got my brother's van, and I went to Kent and told him to bring your shit because I'm not paying for grades like this," remembers his mother. "He told me he'd do better, but I wanted him to pack it in."

They had already paid for another semester, and she was unsure if she could get a refund. "I told him I was giving him one final chance because I wasn't going to pay for Ds and Fs. I told him my money is not going down the tube like that," she said. "I knew he could do the work. When he was in school earlier, he would not do things and then see I wasn't going to put up with it, and it would be amazing how cooperative he would be."

The next semester, James earned his eligibility, eventually making the dean's list with a 3.4 average. While he left school to pursue professional football about a year short of a degree, he would never have academic problems again.

Although he still harbored intense interest in football, his 18-month layoff, with no conditioning, made his 5' 11" frame balloon to almost 270 pounds. His lack of conditioning was exposed during his initial comeback with a new coaching staff. He admits he was often reduced to a heaving, puking mess after early morning workouts. "I was in terrible shape, the worst in my life, no question," he said.

Murgatroyd remembers the new staff mocking him for taking a chance on Harrison.

"Here's James showing up for winter workouts, out of shape, throwing up," he said. It caused Pees and his new coaches to consider him a non-entity, especially since Harrison's demeanor was nothing short of antagonistic.

In reality, it was just another example of his upbringing – the shield – where his shyness and lack of trust caused him to be standoffish and come off, at best, as boorish.

But one thing Murgatroyd noticed in those early days was there was no quit in Harrison.

"While he might have gotten sick when he was out of shape, he always finished," he said. At his worst stage of conditioning, he still looked like a "Greek God."

He also remembers Harrison's honesty. "If I asked him if he went to class, he'd look at me and say 'Coach, I didn't go,' " said Murgatroyd. "He was upfront and honest about things whether you liked it or not."

While he was comfortable with Murgatroyd, the shield that Harrison's mother taught him to create to keep others at bay went up again with the new coaching staff headed by Pees, who was defensive coordinator at Michigan State before taking on the rebuilding task at Kent. Pees and his staff, which included Greg Colby, now head coach at Millersville University in eastern Pennsylvania, were intent on cleaning house, dumping anyone not

During his first year of eligibility at Kent State,
Harrison not only grew up in mind but also in body.

willing to work hard and be exemplary citizens and students off the field.

Pees didn't know about Harrison when he arrived but soon saw a man in terrible shape.

"I wasn't real happy with him at the very beginning, that's for sure. He couldn't finish any of the drills we did in the off-season program. It was a tough program, and a lot of guys didn't make it through, and we ended up getting rid of a lot of them," Pees said. But the coach said he had no preconceptions, giving every-one on the roster a clean slate. "It didn't matter if he was good in the past or bad in the past. We were starting over," he said.

Colby's first impression wasn't very good either. He said Harri-son smelled like he had just finished a smoke when he first came into his office, not exactly part of the new training regimen. It turned out Harrison had just had a mini-cigar.

Colby and Pees, who had coached high school in Ohio and had talked with Tipton about Harrison, were wary but intrigued. "When he walked through the door, he had that look," Colby said, defining it as someone who was very tough and absolutely loved playing football. The reality was that these coaches needed good players, and they thought they might have one in their midst.

The new staff, Murgatroyd included, was tough on Harrison, which he clearly did not like. But as Colby said, "He stuck it out, didn't quit. You could tell the kid had a drive in him." Pees and the others realized once Harrison got into some semblance of shape and entered full-contact practices that he "had a ton of talent," but that he didn't display it every day. But just as his Pee Wee coach had complained to his dad and the Coventry coach almost came to blows with Harrison, Pees had trouble getting him to buy into the new culture he was trying to create.

"Even though he was the best player on the team – he knew it and I knew it – I didn't start him right away," said Pees. "When he wanted to do it, no one could compete with him, but I would not start him until he did everything on and off the field to the best of his ability. It was tough for me as a coach, but I was try-

Harrison wore No. 16 for most of his Kent State career, his dad's number in minor league professional baseball.

ing to establish a program and do it the right way. At that point he wasn't doing it."

One source of friction between Pees and Harrison was the "coaches' table," an intensive, coach-monitored study hall required for those with lagging grades. Because of his earlier academic problems, Harrison was put in the group, which the players playfully called "solitary confinement."

While he didn't like it, Harrison not only endured it, but, according to Pees, it was the reason Harrison earned a 3.4 grade point average during his first semester on the team. Harrison was so elated that he posted his grades on every coach's office chalk boards, which brought a chuckle from Pees many years later.

The coach concluded that Harrison was no dummy; it was just a matter of making him do his work. Harrison would dog it in sprints, not finish all drills and do other things that Pees feared would send a mixed message to his players. Everyone needed to buy into the program, and Harrison wasn't all in unless he was scrimmaging.

Harrison did not like the sprints and other endurance drills. "I hated conditioning, but that shit was hard," he said of why he didn't produce in that area. So he would remain second on the depth chart until he did everything asked of him. That didn't happen, so Harrison was told to find a place on the bench, frustrating the player and his coach.

One Sunday evening, early in the 1999 season, Pees was watching film of a loss the previous day. He saw that Harrison made plays every time he put him into the game, so he called him into his office for a heart-to-heart talk. "You can't be happy sitting on the bench, and I'm not happy to see you sitting on the bench, so we either have to work this out or go our separate ways," the coach told Harrison. If he did everything he was asked to during the next week, Pees told Harrison, he'd put him in 50 percent of the plays. If he did it for two weeks, he'd start.

It turned out James Harrison was listening.

8

Dominating Again

Harrison not only began operating at full speed on the field but also kept up in class.

Physical fitness became his passion. He became the master of the weight room. He got into the best shape of his life, beginning to build the massive arms he now is famous for. By the time he hit his college prime, he weighed 241 pounds and, according to Kent records, had only 7.7 percent body fat, a ridiculously low number for a guy who weighed 30 pounds more just months before.

He credits his coach's forthrightness in the turnaround. "When he told me the way it was, I said, 'All right, I'll do it' and he lived up to his word," Harrison said of Pees. But another stumbling block would emerge before he played his first game. Harrison was afraid to fly. He says he never liked the idea of even getting into an airplane, but once he got to college, he realized that it was a necessity.

The basis of his fear, an issue that plagues him to this day: "They crash," he says curtly.

He was so panicked about flying that his parents drove him to

games instead of him riding on the team plane. An event in his senior year sealed his life-long fear. While his parents drove him to the game, a plane carrying the rest of the Kent team from a game against Northern Illinois almost crashed after birds flew into the engines.

He flies with the Steelers today and other times when there is no alternative. But if he can avoid it, he does, as he did in the summer of 2009 when he refused to go to the White House for a Super Bowl victory celebration and the ESPY awards in Los Angeles, where he was a finalist in three categories.

In 1999, after Pees made him a part-time starter, he recorded 67 tackles, nine for losses, to lead his team. He had four games in which he recorded at least a dozen tackles. In 2000, he recorded 106 tackles, with three sacks, 13 tackles for losses, recovered three fumbles and made an interception. "He was without a doubt the best player on the field," said Murgatroyd. "He was a difference-maker. We created blitzes for him."

Former Steeler defensive coordinator and NFL head coach Dom Capers is a close friend of Murgatroyd. When he saw tape of James, he said he reminded him of former Steelers great Greg Lloyd, who always played better when it got harder to get to the quarterback. Murgatroyd coached at Ohio State, Tennessee and several other schools after leaving Kent and says Harrison would have dominated competition anywhere. "When he lined up, he'd kick the tight end's ass, knocking them around like rag dolls," he said. He also was adept at dropping back into pass coverage, a skill most rush linebackers do not possess.

While scouts would say he wasn't big enough or fast enough to play in the pros, Murgatroyd said no one could block him, and his athleticism stood out. "In fact, I would have played Harrison at running back because he would have been better than most of our running backs," he said.

Among his many victims in college was future NFL star Drew Brees of Purdue, who chastised Harrison, complaining that his ferocity could have injured his knees and hurt his chances of going early in the NFL draft. "I told him as far as I was concerned, the only place he was going was on the ground," Harrison said. Veteran NFL Quarterback Byron Leftwich of Marshall, who played for the Steelers in 2008, also was one of Harrison's sack victims, along with Ben Roethlisberger, his future Steelers teammate.

But there were the familiar rough patches.

"He and I had a couple of run-ins on the field, which caused him to be kicked off the field," Colby said. "I found he doesn't like to be criticized in front of other people. Once I would pull him over to the side to discuss things, it was always 'yes sir, no sir, no problem,' and things began to work out well. It took awhile for him to get some level of trust, but once he did, his attitude was, if the coach wants me to do something, I'm going to do it," said Colby, who became good friends with Harrison as time went on.

Although Harrison is not the fastest linebacker he has coached, like former Illinois stars and NFL players Simeon Rice or Kevin Hardy, Colby said Harrison was the strongest, an instinctive kind of player who made plays you couldn't coach.

While Pees said he would never have dreamed it when he first encountered Harrison, the changes in his work habits and approach so impressed his teammates that they named him captain in his final year. "I thought they felt I could be one of the leaders on the team. I appreciated it," Harrison said of the honor. He never was a rah-rah type of captain, preferring then as now to let his actions speak louder than his words.

The metamorphosis was apparent, Pees said, after Kent lost to Iowa in a blowout early in Harrison's senior year and his defensive captain paid him a visit. "We didn't play good defense, so he came in and told me he shouldn't be captain. He told me he wasn't worthy of the title since they got beat so bad on defense," Pees said. But he refused to accept Harrison's resignation.

Harrison's last year was by far his best. He recorded 98 tackles, 20 tackles for losses, 12 sacks, three interceptions and three forced fumbles. He was named to the All-MAC First Team and earned Kent's defensive player of the year award (named for

Steelers legend Jack Lambert) but placed third in the Mid American Conference award. Ahead of him were linebacker Max Yates of Marshall, who would play in only one game for the San Francisco 49ers, and Brandon Hicks of Bowling Green, a defensive lineman who was on the Indianapolis Colts roster for one year.

The highlight to the year came against perennial league power Miami University of Ohio. Kent had won five of its previous six games and needed a win to cement its first winning season in more than 20 years.

With 2:54 left, and Kent clinging to a 24-20 lead, Miami quarterback Ben Roethlisberger had moved the ball to Kent's 33-yard-line when Harrison, with the help of defensive back Shannon Davis, sacked him for a 7-yard loss.

Harrison was frequently moved around the field to put him in positions to make plays. Pees called a timeout with the game and a winning season on the line against a quarterback who would become a No. 1 draft pick. He moved Harrison to the right side to play against Miami's weakest lineman and told him, "Look, James, you've got to get home." With 1:26 left, Harrison stormed in and sacked Roethlisberger for a 15-yard loss, which gave Kent the ball and the victory. "Roethlisberger never even got set," Pees said.

To this day, Harrison says Roethlisberger occasionally takes credit for the linebacker's NFL career. "He says he's the only reason I'm in the league because he let me sack him," Harrison says of the quarterback's taunts. Harrison says he simply chuckles when he hears those words.

9

Too Slow, Too Small for the NFL?

While he dominated MAC competition from his first start at Kent State, James Harrison was an afterthought to NFL scouts. The two players who placed above him in conference MVP awards were invited to the East-West Shrine All-Star game. Harrison was snubbed.

NFL scouts liked his intensity, but a slow 4.8 seconds in the 40-yard dash (he has since improved it) and his stature relegated him to border-line prospect status. He wasn't even invited to the NFL combine where potential draft picks are evaluated. At best, he was projected as a free agent to fill a training camp roster spot.

"I spoke with NFL guys who asked about him, and the first thing they'd bring up was he was only about 5'11", " said Pees. "I'd tell them he is strong, really quick." The most compelling fact that NFL scouts overlooked, according to Pees, was that "no one could knock him off his feet." While he wasn't sure whether Harrison would fit into various NFL defensive schemes, he told anyone who asked that this guy could "just play ball."

Parise, who has been an NFL agent for 25 years, says he watched tape of Harrison while checking out another player and found him to be "one of the best linebackers I've ever seen in my life. I called the kid I was representing (Josh Bostik, who didn't make it in the NFL) and said, 'Who is that No.16?' He said that's James Harrison!" Parise asked Bostik to tell Harrison he was available. However, they wouldn't come together until years later.

When the scouts looked into his background, the issues from high school, now five years old, came up again, along with his penchant for communication problems with coaches until he got to know them. His dour demeanor, long used as a shield for shyness, once again worked against him. It was something he would work to overcome to make it in the NFL.

"When I was younger," he says now, "it was my anger that was my natural reaction to something, whatever it may be. I wasn't going to cry about things. I was going to answer things with my fists. Now that I'm a little older and wiser, off the field I can control that and brush it off with comments like 'They're ignorant,' when he hears race-baiting, or 'They're too young and dumb to realize what they're doing.' "

By draft day, he knew he would be bypassed, but he was encouraged that several teams, including the Steelers, were prepared to offer him a free agent contract. He knew the odds were at least 100,000-to-1 to make the NFL. He knew there were 32 teams in the NFL, 53 on a roster, meaning only 1,696 are part of this elite fraternity, with only 22 players on the field in a game at a time.

He knew all the perceptions NFL scouts had about him. He knew the draft day selections with their hefty bonuses would be given preference over free agents. But no matter what they said, he knew in his heart he could play at the NFL level. In fact, Harrison never believed he was a long shot. Looking back at it, he says, "I thought if I got the opportunity, even if it was to play special teams, once I made a team, I knew I'd show them I could play."

And he never put any stock in his perceived deficiencies. "A guy that looks good in a non-contact drill like running 40 yards is one thing. But when you put the pads on, you've got to see who can hold up. When it comes down to it, it's about the speed of the game, not whether you've got guys who can run up and down the field. If a linebacker has to run 40 yards during a play, you ain't doing what you need to be doing."

Of course, Harrison would be proven wrong on that point in Super Bowl XLIII when he would be forced to run more than 100 yards for a touchdown.

10

The First Cut
Isn't the Deepest

W hen he took a $4,000 bonus and signed a free agent contract with the Steelers, all James Harrison wanted was a chance. Why Pittsburgh? "That was the team that wanted me," he said, "so that's why I came." The Oakland Raiders were the other eager suitor.

Mike Archer, a former head coach at LSU who has worked as a major college defensive coordinator, was the Steelers linebackers coach at the time. Before Harrison arrived, he had coached an extraordinary linebacking corps that included Kevin Greene, Greg Lloyd, Levon Kirkland, Earl Holmes, Jason Gildon, Chad Brown and Joey Porter.

As the 2002 draft was coming to a close, Steelers Director of Football Operations Kevin Colbert and his staff focused on the free agents they would sign. The team was interested in a cornerback from Miami University of Ohio and called his agent. As Archer remembers it, the agent crafted a package free agent deal. "He said he'd get the corner for us if we took James Harrison, so I grabbed some film of him at Kent State and saw a guy running around making plays, a very active guy who was very aggressive and seemed like he was having fun playing." So Archer persuaded Colbert to bring Harrison into camp.

Harrison neatly fit the two criteria for a Steeler linebacker: He made plays and was extremely physical. Harrison was told to report at 6 p.m. the next day for physicals and the subsequent rookie camp. But, at the appointed hour, Harrison was nowhere to be found. "Coach Cowher was asking me, 'Where the ….. is Harrison?' " Archer recalled.   "I thought he was going to fire me."

They finally tracked him down at his parents' house in Akron. He told Archer he didn't know when he was supposed to re-port but that he'd be there in the two hours it takes to drive from Akron. Harrison said it was a misunderstanding, but he also remembers encountering none other than Cowher – who was headed home for the day – in the parking lot on his arrival. The head coach was not happy. "That's how it started. It had its rough moments," Archer said.

Even though his bonus was one of the lowest offered by the team, Harrison thought he was rich. It enabled him to replace his old motorcycle with a newer 750 Suzuki. Once he got his schedule right, Harrison, like most rookies, had difficulty learning the complicated Steelers defense, which was much more com-plex than anything he'd seen in college. Part of that complexity was the imperative that every player understand not only his own role, but also those of everyone around him.

Following the now familiar pattern, Harrison came off as surly just as he had in the past with coaches he had not yet become comfortable with. But there was a big difference in the NFL: That kind of demeanor is usually the prescription for failure.

Because the defense was hard to learn, Archer would show plays on tape and ask players what they should do. Harrison's responses were curt and often borderline condescending toward his coach. If that continued, for Harrison, "NFL would have meant 'Not For Long,' " Archer said.

While he was a few minutes late for meetings here and there, which Archer called "typical rookie transgressions," he eventually

James Harrison records his first sack on Cleveland Browns
Quarterback Jeff Garcia on Nov. 14, 2004. He was thrust into
his first career start after All-Pro linebacker Joey Porter was
ejected before the game started. Harrison finished with six
tackles and made a variety of other outstanding plays in his
Steeler debut as a starter.

James Harrison with football immortal Jim Brown after a home game with Cleveland.

The only speed for James
Harrison on the football
field is full speed.

Harrison makes a play against Cincinnati.

came on board just as he had in high school and college. Harrison was never a braggart and never said much, but Archer would learn that his sullen, somewhat threatening demeanor masked his bashfulness. "Of course, he was around Joey Porter, so he knew how to talk smack," Archer laughed.

The other compelling dimension to Harrison's personality was his dignity and pride. "It bothered him when he couldn't answer a question, so he reacted negatively. I think it was his pride," Archer said. Years later, that pride would overcome all of the negatives, making Harrison the outstanding player he is today.

Harrison's gruff, impolite approach didn't last long. "I think it was Joey Porter who told him when he's in that room, don't give the coach a bunch of shit, and that's how it started, how he learned how to become a professional," Archer said.

Another star player who helped him was Gildon, an All-Pro linebacker at the time and now renowned as one of the greatest Steeler linebackers ever. "We always knew he had the ability to play at this level, but sometimes guys coming in from smaller schools really don't realize the chance they have until it is too late," he said.

Gildon said Harrison got caught up looking at the numbers early on, figuring he had at best a slim chance of making the team, which affected his confidence. "He showed the ability. He just had to go out there and believe he could play," his former teammate said.

Harrison didn't react well to criticism, covering up his lack of knowledge in meetings with a somewhat menacing persona.

"He was young, he wanted to have the correct answers, so when he didn't, he'd act angry. It was his mechanism to cover it up, and he didn't want to appear soft," Gildon said.

But on the field, that attitude was the one Steelers linebackers have historically exhibited with great success. "You have to have a certain disposition to play that position for the Pittsburgh Steelers, and he was trying to fit in as best he could," Gildon said.

When Harrison played, he showed he fit in, even though he was cut four times over a two-year span. Despite that, Gildon said everyone thought Harrison had the ability to play in the NFL. "I didn't think it was the last we would see of him," he said of the cuts.

Gildon left the Steelers before Harrison finally made it, playing the last season of his storied career in Jacksonville, but he kept in touch with his former teammates. "They were all telling me how well he'd been doing, which made sense because he finally realized what he had to do as a pro to make it in the NFL and to make it as a Pittsburgh Steeler linebacker. He stepped right in after Joey (Porter) left," he said. "From the beginning, he definitely had the talent to play, but he was like a lot of people who don't realize there's more to this game than going out there on Sunday."

Gildon still relishes his time with what he calls his "Band of Brothers" in the Steelers linebacker corps. Now he says its leader is quickly becoming Harrison. He hopes the guy he tried to help carries on the legacy. "James has definitely made his mark as another great linebacker for the Steelers. At this point, I hope he takes on one of the things I've always tried to pride myself on: Since something was given to me, the legacy of the Steelers is to pass it on to the younger guys.

"He's at the top. Now he has to reach back to help those younger guys elevate their games, to keep it strong," Gildon said. He said Greg Lloyd and Kevin Greene played that role for him.

He says the way the players at the top of their games help those at the bottom of the depth charts sets apart teams like the Steelers who are successful year in and year out. "That's one of the things that keeps the Steelers on top because the bottom line is winning, regardless of who is out there in the starting role. We all win like we all lose, and we're only as strong as our weakest link," said Gildon, a father of four, who is considering getting into coaching.

One thing Harrison was right about was the competition for a job against the best linebacker corps in the NFL. "There was no doubt about how explosive he was," Archer said, comparing him favorably to Lloyd and Kendrell Bell, 2001 defensive rookie of the year. "You could see it in individual drills. He wasn't the tallest guy, but he had leverage that he has always used as an advantage."

After he left the Steelers, Archer remembers watching a Baltimore game in which Harrison uprooted and drove backward 11-time pro bowler Jonathan Ogden, who is 6-foot-9 inches tall and weighs 345 pounds. Like his high school and college coaches, Archer said, "There was nobody who could block him."

The first big break Harrison got came during the last 2002 preseason game, against the Lions in Detroit. Gildon had a sore knee, so backup Clark Haggans was set to play most of the snaps but got hurt early in the game. That left the team with no alternative but to play the free agent rookie fighting for a job. It would not be the last time that a Haggans' injury would change the course of Harrison's career. "He played almost the entire game

Mildred Harrison enjoys a laugh with Jerome Bettis after a Steeler
victory.

and played very well," Archer said.

Harrison knew he was going to get some mop-up time in Detroit but didn't realize he'd play almost every down. "I remember the next day, my whole body hurt" from the most extensive action he'd had in over a year.

That put the Steelers in something of a bind. They had solid linebackers with no real need for another, but Cowher and Colbert were concerned that, if they cut Harrison, he'd quickly get plucked from the waiver wire. Plus, they all knew Harrison was a potentially great special teams player, willing to give up his body to break up the wedge designed to spring loose kick returners. Because Cowher coached special teams, his interest in Harrison was great.

Despite all this, they took a chance and cut him, hoping the negatives of Harrison's size and speed would dissuade others. They were right. Harrison was signed as a practice squad player the next day. Shortly thereafter, they learned Harrison had suffered a debilitating hand injury early in the Detroit game but played anyway and played well. Playing with such intense pain "tells you something about him right there," Archer said. Harrison not only practiced every day with the swollen hand but also spent hours in the weight room trying to do exercises with one hand.

Archer said he ordered him and Bell to meet with him at 7 each morning to discuss and learn the defense. Harrison didn't think he needed that because he was a practice squad player whose role was to play on the scout team each week. "I told him I didn't care if he didn't want to do it, even if he hated me for it," Archer said. "I didn't care if he hated me or not. I told him it was my job to make him better."

While he has heard Harrison does not like him, he said while on a recruiting trip in 2008 he stopped in at Steelers headquarters and was given a welcoming reception by players he had worked with. As he chatted with a newspaper reporter, he noticed Harrison in the background, patiently waiting until the conversation ended. Harrison stepped up and greeted him warmly, something he appreciates to this day. "What a lot of people don't realize because of his demeanor when he buckles up the chin strap is that he has a good side to him, too," Archer said.

He said the early morning sessions definitely helped Harrison learn the complicated defense, which paid off before his first year ended. The team suffered an inordinate number of injuries late in the 2002 season, forcing them to activate Harrison for the final three games and the playoffs.

Archer left the Steelers after that season, but he said Harrison was well on his way to learning the entire defense and was fast building the mindset needed to be a linebacker for the Pittsburgh Steelers. The credit for that, according to Archer, goes to the other linebackers, including Porter, Gildon and James Farrior, who took him under their wing. "I saw him slowly starting to change to become a professional," Archer said. Porter, who had a difficult time adjusting to the rigors of professional football early in his career, once told Archer he saw a lot of himself in Harrison.

As Archer sees it, Harrison is one of the greatest examples of a relentless will to succeed he has ever encountered. "For people to never quit until they have success, he's a classic example."

For his part, Harrison said he was under no illusions about his chances, given the complexities of the schemes, the speed of the pro game, the extraordinary strength exhibited by the players and the overall intensity of the game. "You got to come in and do something to make them look at you and say, 'Well, there's something in that guy that we can use,' " he said.

As for the personal raps he has endured since he was a child, where people called him uncoachable, sullen, angry, distant and intimidating if not downright mean, he figured if he just continued to be himself, everything would be all right. "I guess my natural look might be mean because I'm not smiling or laughing all the time. I'm not trying to look that way or scare anyone, but I can't help that. I'm not going to sit there and smile all day to make you feel comfortable," he said.

He admits the complicated NFL defenses slowed him down him for a while, but says the reason he didn't stick for good at the outset was an initial lack of opportunity because of the draftees who get huge signing bonuses. "If you get a guy who is a first- or a second-round pick, he's going to get a year, maybe two or maybe three years to develop. If you get a guy who's not draft- ed, if he doesn't come into camp and do something spectacular, he may not have the opportunity to play on special teams or be on the practice squad," he said.

While he rarely dwells on those days, occasionally he talks about what it took to make it. "Everybody in the NFL says it isn't about where you're from but about where you're at. I always thought if it isn't about where you're from, then why I am sitting behind people I outplayed?" he said.

With the NFL's collective bargaining agreement set to expire in 2010, Harrison believes it should adopt a rookie salary cap like the NBA and NHL. Such a system would stop the burgeoning first-round rookie bonus payments that sap teams of money they could spend on core veterans like himself. It would particularly benefit well-managed teams like the Steelers.

The overriding positive from his first year: Harrison found out he was good enough to play in the NFL. While he had become a physical fitness and weightlifting zealot, he also realized he could succeed only if he continued to transform his body into a chis- eled mass that would continue to make him as unblockable as he was in high school and college. Today, his workout regimen is extremely intensive and keeps him among the most conditioned and strongest players in the NFL.

One thing he didn't discard, though, was that shield, which his agent Parise said had an impact on his first stint with the Steel- ers. "When he stared at them during discussions, he'd scare the hell out of them," the agent said.

Whatever the reasons, after a year on the practice squad and a bit part as a part-time special teams player, Harrison was on the outside looking in.

Harrison overcame problems with coaches like Mike Archer, a former Steelers linebacker coach, to finally make it in the NFL.

Harrison, with former Steeler Larry Foote behind him, sees the sky's the limit.

11

I Can Play in the NFL?

Harrison was in the best shape of his life at the beginning of his second year. He began to understand the Steelers defensive system. He was prepared to give up his body on special teams and learn linebacker assignments at every position.

Harrison made the team's active roster on a Monday but was cut two days later because NFL rules prohibit players from spending more than a year on the practice squads. The Steelers instead signed a linebacker named Eric Flowers, a first-round pick of the Buffalo Bills two years earlier, who was cut despite his lofty draft status. The Steelers thought they were getting a deal but quickly found out Buffalo had legitimate reasons for letting him go.

Once they discarded Flowers, Harrison was signed and cut again in a three-week period, again a victim of the Steelers numbers game. He found himself once again on the Pennsylvania Turnpike headed back to Akron with a stoic attitude but wondering whether his dream of playing professional football was coming to an end.

For the rest of that season, a frustrated Harrison watched as other linebackers who had never made a professional roster were signed ahead of him by teams all over the NFL.

"There was something like a dozen linebackers who got hurt, and James never got a call," remembers his dad.

That's when he learned his agents – who get paid only when a player makes a team – were not even shopping his services. So he fired them and hired Parise on the advise of one of his old Kent teammates. Parise not only remains his agent to this day, but also has become his confidant in Pittsburgh, where Parise is based.

Parise remembered the college tape he'd seen of Harrison and was still impressed. He did not know Harrison but figured when he got the call he would meet a player depressed from being cut so much. Harrison was still under a representation agreement, so under NFL rules, he had to fire the other agents before he could sign with Parise.

Harrison called them a few times but got no return messages. He didn't want to leave a message firing them, but his mom, re-prising her childhood precepts to her son, told him to simply call and tell whoever answered the phone that they were done. "I told him if he didn't call, I would. I was going to tell him if you ain't got the time to talk to James, you don't have the time to represent him," Mildred Harrison said. Eventually, Harrison got in touch with the agents and dismissed them.

Like most people Harrison encountered, Parise saw a lack of trust that lessened when the new agent made clear that he takes a hands-on approach to the players he represents.

"I told him I'll follow through on everything, no matter if you are cut or whatever," he said. "I told him if you're with me, you're with me until we mutually decide it's over."

It didn't hurt that Harrison also met Parise's wife, Linda, who quickly became a maternal presence for him.

Parise grew up in Butler, where he is a member of the Butler High School Athletic Hall of Fame. He did his undergraduate and graduate studies at the University of New Mexico, where he starred as a gymnast. He had seen tape of Harrison at Kent, but did not know Harrison before going to work for him. While he is director of the sprawling Beaver County YMCA – which he raised $11 million to build – he has represented professional football and track athletes for the past 25 years.

Also a personal trainer, Parise said he found a flaw in Harrison's running form in one of the first workouts the player did, enabling him to cut his time in the 40-yard-dash by nearly .3 of a second, making him as fast as most NFL linebackers.

Looking back on Harrison's year-and-a-half effort to make the Steelers roster, Parise couldn't understand why the team didn't embrace his new client. Harrison looked great in scrimmages. He'd done exceptionally well when he was forced to fill in during the preseason in Detroit. But he found out the coaches thought he wasn't learning the defensive system quickly enough or thought he wasn't committed to learning it. He had been late to practice and late to a few meetings. He was also not as big as the Steelers wanted a linebacker to be or fast enough.

"He ran like a duck, but once we got him straightened out, he was fine," Parise said. "The bottom line is that he has a lot of horsepower. When he pushes, things happen. People go backwards." Yet the agent realized Harrison was not shaped like other Steelers linebackers who were routinely 6-3, 245 pounds.   "He didn't fit the mold," Parise said. "The fact that he was not a great conversationalist was also a negative, but, on the positive side, when he was on the field, he dominated."

Parise acknowledges that initial encounters with Harrison can be off-putting. But he was able to pierce that facade to find the thoughtful, bright, engaging man underneath. Along with helping Harrison develop physically, Parise embarked on a program to help him overcome the negatives NFL types had saddled him with. The message got through to Harrison: If he wanted to play professional football, he had to clear up the personality issues.

As the 2003 season was coming to an end, Parise at first couldn't find a place for Harrison, but then brokered a deal with the Bal-

Harrison handles the wheel of a boat during a deep water fishing trip during his visit to Hawaii for the 2009 Pro Bowl.

timore Ravens for a roster spot that would open after Harrison went to Germany to play in the ill-fated NFL Europe. "They told me they were going to take him but feared he was not a team guy, had a surly attitude," Parise said. "I told them that was not true. I told them everybody likes him. I told them he never had a problem with teammates, but I admitted some coaches were scared to death of him until they got to know him."

Parise spent a lot of time talking to Harrison about changing his demeanor, especially with folks he did not know very well. He said the root of it was his basic principle that there is no gray area in life. "James is a standup guy. He won't back down to anything. If he's wrong, he's wrong. That's the way it is, and I've never met anyone stronger than James in those convictions,"

Parise said.

Going to Germany to play for $500 a week was the last thing Harrison wanted to do. To start with, he would have to fly there. In addition, he had no desire to move to a foreign country. He wasn't sure there was a place for him on the linebacker-rich Ravens either.

"Bill, I ain't going," he told Parise. "Yes, you are, James," replied the agent. "You've got to go." The argument lasted until the player boarded the plane.

Parise knew that if NFL types saw Harrison play, they'd realize he was a top-flight talent. The first stop was southwest Florida where all the NFL Europe teams trained. Parise stopped in for a few days and said after practices and a series of scrimmages, it was clear to him and just about everyone he talked to that Harrison was the best player there.

12

Flying to NFL Europe as a Raven

While he would play only four games, Harrison quickly became a star in NFL Europe, known as the "little guy," who, as in his college days, made an impact on almost every play. Parise figured his performance for the Rhein Fire in Germany would catapult him back into the NFL.

He would earn defensive player of the week awards and plaudits from players, coaches and commentators for his hard-hitting play, whether it was as an outside linebacker in a 4-3 scheme (the Steelers run a 3-4 defense) or as a special teams player.

In one game, announcers Kevin Slaton and Jason Garrett watched in awe as Harrison made play after play against the Berlin Thunder. Harrison hurt his left knee in the first half while making a block during an interception return but stormed back to make numerous tackles, record a sack and make plays on special teams.

Garrett was impressed. "Harrison has been all over the place... he's playing great on special teams, too, something NFL teams will see, and I'm sure James Harrison knows that as well," he said on a television broadcast.

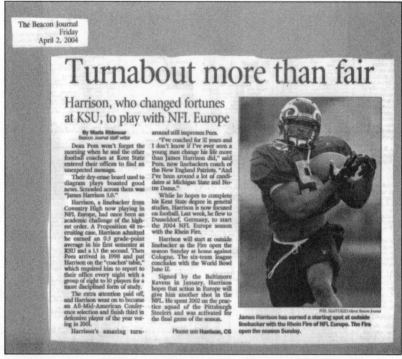

The Beacon Journal
Friday
April 2, 2004

Turnabout more than fair

Harrison, who changed fortunes at KSU, to play with NFL Europe

By Marla Ridenour
Beacon Journal staff writer

Dean Pees won't forget the morning when he and the other football coaches at Kent State entered their offices to find an unexpected message.

Their dry-erase board used to diagram plays boasted good news. Scrawled across them was "James Harrison 3.0."

Harrison, a linebacker from Coventry High now playing in NFL Europe, had once been an academic challenge of the highest order. A Proposition 48 recruiting case, Harrison admitted he earned an 0.5 grade-point average in his first semester at KSU and a 1.5 the second. Then Pees arrived in 1998 and put Harrison on the "coaches' table," which required him to report to their office every night with a group of eight to 10 players for a more disciplined form of study.

The extra attention paid off, and Harrison went on to become an All-Mid-American Conference selection and finish third in defensive player of the year voting in 2001.

Harrison's amazing turn-around still impresses Pees.

"I've coached for 32 years and I don't know if I've ever seen a young man change his life more than James Harrison did," said Pees, now linebackers coach of the New England Patriots. "And I've been around a lot of candidates at Michigan State and Notre Dame."

While he hopes to complete his Kent State degree in general studies, Harrison is now focused on football. Last week, he flew to Dusseldorf, Germany, to start the 2004 NFL Europe season with the Rhein Fire.

Harrison will start at outside linebacker as the Fire open the season Sunday at home against Cologne. The six-team league concludes with the World Bowl June 12.

Signed by the Baltimore Ravens in January, Harrison hopes that action in Europe will give him another shot in the NFL. He spent 2002 on the practice squad of the Pittsburgh Steelers and was activated for the final game of the season.

Please see Harrison, C6

PHIL MASTURZO/Akron Beacon Journal

James Harrison has earned a starting spot at outside linebacker with the Rhein Fire of NFL Europe. The Fire open the season Sunday.

There is almost nothing Harrison liked about Europe but the NFL games in which he showed he could play well in a professional setting.

As Harrison was toiling on a muddy soccer field in Europe that day, across the Atlantic the NFL draft was taking place. Players like quarterbacks Eli Manning, Philip Rivers and Ben Roethlisberger, his future teammate, were being selected in the first round. Like Roethlisberger in college, as time moved forward, both of those other high-priced quarterbacks would be victims of Harrison sacks.

As always, Harrison loved playing the games, even if they were on bad surfaces before sparse crowds. Off the field, Harrison was miserable. While he was used to racism in America, it was worse in Germany. He and his teammates were repeatedly accosted by people of various nationalities in clubs who had no use for interloping football players.

In one instance, one of his teammates got into an argument with a man who turned out to be a member of a Turkish Mafia organization. When the football player pushed the aggressor out of his way, the Turks, who sometimes carried guns, locked the club's doors and told the Americans, "We're going to send you back to the states in pine boxes." They were able to get away before anything happened.

In general, Harrison said there was little he liked. He could not understand the language, didn't like the food and was more than a bit homesick. His mom bought international phone cards that enabled her to talk with her son almost every day. "It was so bad over there, so dangerous, that I thought James might never come back," said the woman reared on the mean streets of Akron, who doesn't like to fly either.

Parise said Harrison would call and yell at him every chance he got. He basically stayed in his room, which he considered a hovel compared with American hotels. There were numerous power outages, which forced Harrison and other hotel visitors to sit in the hallways until the lights were restored.

The minor knee injury he sustained against Berlin worsened, resulting in Harrison's ticket back to the States. Harrison was sent to an NFL Europe rehab facility in Alabama. He was in no hurry to return to Germany, allowing his rehab to last three weeks, which brought the season to a close. "It wasn't a serious knee injury," Parise said. "He would play with it now, but he damn sure wasn't going back."

While it was clear the Ravens weren't thrilled that Harrison didn't complete the season, he headed to Baltimore with hopes of proving himself – just as he had at Kent State and the Steelers for a time. But Harrison was at the Ravens camp for only a couple of days and got on the field for two plays in a practice before he was sent on his way again.

While he never asked why, he learned later the team needed another tight end and signed Todd Wilcox, a teammate in Europe, instead of Harrison.

"Every time they cut me, they'd ask me if I wanted an explanation. I told them if it isn't going to change the decision, then I don't really need to hear it," he said.

Through the cuts he'd suffered, he watched other players sob and beg coaches for another chance, but that is not the Harrison way. "If it happens, it happens. There is nothing I can do about a decision that someone else makes. Nothing I can do about it... I'm certainly not going to cry about it."

Parise, who has witnessed the gamut of emotions from players cut from NFL rosters, said Harrison was as stoic as anyone he's encountered. "I told him not to worry, that I was going to find a place for him," Parise said. "He said, 'I'm not worried. I know you will.' and that was it." When Parise continued to console him, he remembers how the player reacted: "He told me I was afraid, and that's a sign of weakness," Parise said. He told the agent who was a star high school and college athlete and successful businessman for years: "You're weak, Bill!"

That reaction showed Parise a lot about the player who would become closer to him and his wife Linda than any other person he has represented. "He helped me to understand that just because things aren't right doesn't mean you can't accomplish what you want," he said. "He has a realization of life where he has this ability to never give up. It's an unbelievable resolve, an ability to make himself do anything if he's convinced it's the right thing to do."

Harrison was once again back in Akron hoping to sign with another team, but starting to consider the grim reality of his future. While he continued to work out and by no means had given up on professional football, he began considering a day-time job, such as driving a bus, which he did for a time for Kent State's transportation services, or possibly behind the wheel of a truck like his dad.

"It wasn't the end of the world. I wasn't giving up on professional football, but the worst thing that would happen is that I'd have to go get a job like everyone else," he said.

Whether it was Harrison's reputation, his size or speed, Parise could not find him a job until news reports in Pittsburgh revealed Haggans, the same Steeler linebacker whose injury gave Harrison a preseason chance two years earlier, broke some fingers in a weight room accident just days before the 2003 training camp. Parise asked the Steelers if they'd like to bring Harrison back for a third try.

The agent had only one demand: "I told them James would sign if they guaranteed me that they'd play him in the preseason and not simply cut him as soon as Clark got healthy," Parise said. The Steelers were initially non-committal but agreed the next day. "I knew he would find a place because he was just too good. He always dominated people," Parise said.

Harrison was uncertain if he was ever going to get a chance, but he knew one thing with certainty: "I could play this game. I was just waiting for the opportunity."

James Harrison with Dick LeBeau after he accepted the award as Associated Press NFL Defensive Player of the year in Kansas City.

13

Last Chance
for Harrison (Again)

By the time he signed his fourth free agent contract in the summer of 2004, Harrison had spent two years meandering in and out of Steelers and Ravens training camps. Along the way, he was getting stronger and gaining the confidence to begin playing with his trademark all-out intensity, but all he had to show for it was a few games as a Steelers special team player. His time was so brief, it didn't qualify for a year's service in the NFL pension plan.

What he did know was that it was time to put up or shut up. In media reports prior to this last chance, fellow linebacker James Farrior spoke the plain truth about Harrison. While he was a monster hitter and virtually unblockable when focused on his responsibilities, there were times when the young linebacker was so unsure of himself, he would back off and give up on plays. There was no place for uncertainty in the NFL.

In the past, when Harrison was hesitant, he would revert to that shield his mother taught him to use in West Akron to ward off the outside world. Those retrenchments had long caused coaches to initially question his attitude, his acumen and his intelligence, not to mention the fear he instilled in them. But this time his agent had lengthy discussions with Harrison about his approach to others. Harrison listened to what Parise and his linebacker teammates had to say about life in the NFL and what it takes to be a professional football player.

This time he learned and played every linebacker position at camp and thrived on special teams, making the case that, as he put it later, "If they cut me, I knew I did everything I could do. My whole thing was I wanted to prove them wrong. Did I think the whole world was out to get me? No. I figured if I got better than I was, and continued to improve, I'm fine with that. The difference was maturity. I handled things differently than my rookie year. The way I took to coaching, the way I talked to coaches... that was all different. I had to change all of that because it was basically the last hurrah," he said.

It turned out to be the first of many happy returns. "He was not going to have any negatives," Parise said. "This time he had the confidence to really play at his speed – full speed – rather than the more conservative speed he was playing at before because he often wasn't certain about what to do."

One person who had never seen him before was Dick LeBeau, who had left the Steelers to become a head coach in Cincinnati and returned to coach Pittsburgh's defense when he lost his job. As summer camp began, he watched the force and intensity of a short-statured linebacker no one could block, asking a nearby coach: "Who is number 92?" He was told the name was James Harrison, and he'd been cut four times. Replied LeBeau: "I think his searching for a job days are over. I haven't seen anybody even slow him down."

LeBeau said he'd heard inklings of the supposed baggage Harrison brought with him. But throughout his storied career, he always "tried not to pay attention to anything but what a player does in front of me. I've found over the years it works better to evaluate what you see, not what you hear." What he saw was a tough player who didn't show any hesitation and couldn't be blocked. Off the field, he noticed Harrison lifting weights, studying video, taking his profession very seriously.

Then and now, LeBeau says Harrison is a delight to be around despite the tough-looking façade. "I've never in any way had any confrontational situations with him on anything," LeBeau said. As for his intimidating behavior on the field, "I'm not sure you are going to start your church choir with him, but he's a tough, excellent football player," Le Beau said, joking, "I do think he can sing a bit. That face you're seeing is just a competitive face. He's a focused athlete. What he does is usually not done with a smile on his face. It's not a social setting."

As he got to know Harrison, the coach found a "very intelligent man with a good sense of humor, a tremendous work ethic." Downplaying his role in Harrison's success, LeBeau said, "I was blessed the way he fell to me. If anything, all we did is give him the chance to perform."

For his part, Harrison cherishes his relationship with LeBeau more than anyone in the organization, save Dan Rooney, the team's leader even after he left in 2009 to become U.S. Ambassador to Ireland. LeBeau feels the same way: "He's done so much more for me than what I've done for him. He really appreciates what he has. He has really proven that he's one of the best and to me he's really proven that he's going to be a better football player in the future and that is not just lip service. He's going to do it."

Harrison has the ultimate compliment for his defensive coordinator. "He's a guy I trust," he said. He characterizes LeBeau as "a great coach, almost like a father figure. If coach LeBeau says to do something, I'm going to do it. I don't question him because I trust him," Harrison says. LeBeau, he says, doesn't play favorites either. "He doesn't treat one guy differently than anyone else. He would give me and other veterans the same respect as an undrafted free agent in his rookie year," he said. He said he will carry with him for the rest of his life LeBeau's almost daily pronouncement to his players: "It's a good day to be alive."

Going into 2004, the Steelers had a string of winning but unremarkable seasons since their 1995 Super Bowl XXX loss to the Dallas Cowboys. The Cowher-coached team had been one of the NFL's most successful organizations for more than a decade, making the playoffs 10 times and advancing to the AFC Championship game on six occasions. But Cowher had his worst record during injury-plagued 2003, finishing 6-10, then opening 1-1 in 2004 when Tommy Maddox, the starting quarterback, went down with a neck injury that left him temporarily paralyzed.

That opened the door for Ben Roethlisberger, the 11th pick in the 2004 draft, who was not expected to leave the bench his first year. With a stingy defense and a run-oriented offense that limited the chances for the rookie quarterback to make mistakes, Pittsburgh ran off 14 straight wins to finish 15-1, becoming the first AFC team ever to win that many games. The Steelers made it to the AFC Championship, but fell once again to the New England Patriots, the eventual Super Bowl champion.

A bit player on that team, Harrison built his reputation as a no-nonsense special teams guy who thought nothing of propelling his body into a wall of blockers at full speed. During that time, he carried around his frayed Rhein Fire equipment bag from NFL Europe as a constant reminder of where he'd been and how far he'd come. "It was a reminder of everything I went through and what I didn't want to have to go through again," Harrison said.

On Nov. 14, 2004, Harrison's hometown team Cleveland figured in his first breakthrough, but it took a fluke situation to thrust him into the starting line-up only 10 minutes before the first snap. His trash-talking teammate Joey Porter was doing some taunting at midfield as both teams warmed up. A Browns running back came rushing in to confront Porter. It ended with each being accused of spitting on the other. Both players were ejected before the game even started.

And so with no fanfare, James Harrison would get his first start. His parents didn't even go to the game because his mom didn't like to sit at the top of stadiums, where the Browns put Steelers family members, and they figured he'd only play special teams and mop-up roles. His dad instead went to a neighborhood club for its annual Browns-Steelers party. "I put all my Steeler stuff on and went down there to give it to the Browns fans," James Sr. said.

As the game approached, one of the kids called to say James was starting, so he rushed home to find an excited collection of Harrison siblings. "He showed them what he could do. Everybody was screaming and hollering," James Sr. said. He remembers yelling back at the television when commentators said his son's short stature did not fit the mold of a Steelers linebacker. "I said where did they get that mold from?"

While Harrison knew the plays, he was scared and nervous but excited when the coaches told him he was taking Porter's place. It took a few plays for the adrenalin to wear off, but after Harrison settled down, he put in a masterful performance, piling up six tackles, a sack, and narrowly missing another sack of quarterback Jeff Garcia in the end zone that would have caused a safety.

Harrison did his first live Pittsburgh television interview after the game, telling Stan Savran of "Sports Beat" that when he had Garcia in his sights, he sought the trifecta of a sack, a fumble and recovery for a touchdown. "I wanted it all and came up with nothing," he told the Pittsburgh audience with a smile, betraying no sign that such appearances make him extremely nervous. The next shot he got at the Browns quarterback, he made sure to put him down for his first NFL sack. Later, he would contribute thousands of dollars to a kids program based on his sack totals.

Harrison's play caused a change of thinking among the Steelers coaching staff, some of whom had considered him only a tough-guy special teams player. But LeBeau had already realized they had a quality football player of vast potential. He figured all Harrison needed was a chance. His performance cemented his status. "He played an excellent game," LeBeau said. "From that day forward, I was sure we had an excellent player."

Harrison's progress was not lost on Cowher. During his weekly media gathering, he said: "James Harrison is a good football player. We have played him inside, we played him outside. He has been an integral part of the kicking game. He has taken a very professional approach. From the time he came here his first year to where he is right now, he prepares. The attention to detail, little things, it is important to him. He is a very explosive guy. If you talk to anybody on the team, pound for pound, he may be one of the strongest guys on the team. He is an explosive hitter who can run. He did a great job the other day stepping in for Joey, he really did," the coach said.

While it was his first taste of success outside of special teams play, and while he would recover a fumble for his first NFL touchdown against Buffalo on the last day of the regular season, he still didn't feel like he had made it. He still hoarded his money, never knowing when it would be cut off. He still rented an apartment in Pittsburgh's North Hills, not wanting to purchase a house he couldn't afford if he was cut again.

As in childhood, he never veered far from his mother. But he became closer and more dependent on his agent Bill Parise and wife Linda, visiting their Beaver County home on off days and having dinner with them at least once a week. "I just think he needed someone here that could help him, who he could pick up a phone and call," said Linda Parise, reflecting on the player's shyness and insecurities. Plus, he liked her cooking.

As their relationship grew, Harrison would rely on the Parises to help him through many problems – big and small – as they became his Pittsburgh anchors. Whether it was help with a flat tire or simply a home-cooked meal, Bill and Linda provided for Harrison whenever they could, building a rare trusting relationship outside the player's family.

While there were no guarantees about his career, by his account and that of LeBeau, he was getting better every day. Most of all, he was starting to believe he would finally get the chance to play on a regular basis. When the opportunity came along, he was determined to make the most of it.

The 2005 season began with promise, with the Steelers winning seven of their first nine games. Then Roethlisberger and

Charlie Batch, his back-up, went down with injuries, thrusting Maddox back into the lineup. Harrison was starting to get a few reps in certain defensive packages, but the All-Pro Porter, with his big contract, still commanded the majority of defensive plays, even if some in Pittsburgh believed he had lost a step.

The Maddox-led team lost to Baltimore, and then after Roethlisberger's return, dropped games to undefeated Indianapolis and Cincinnati in a three-week span. With playoff hopes dimming, the Steelers won the final four regular season games to sneak into the playoffs as a sixth seed, meaning it would have to play every playoff game on the road. No team had ever survived such a daunting path to the Super Bowl.

While he spent most of the year on special teams, he made a mark on his teammates in Cleveland – and on YouTube – during a crucial game two days after Christmas in Cleveland. During a stop in play, a drunken Browns fan raced onto the field toward the Steelers.

He grabbed the drunk around the waist, lifted him up and spiked him to the ground. As Harrison held him on the ground awaiting security personnel, the guy grabbed Harrison's face mask, "looked up at me and said 'Now I got your ass,' " Harrison laughed. "I said 'You do?' "

Later, he was asked why he confronted the Browns fan as he approached running back Verron Haynes from behind. "I didn't know what his plans were, but I wasn't about to wait long enough to find out," he said.

Playing against the Browns was momentous not only because he would get his first start against them a year earlier, but also because he grew up watching them. He cried as an 8-year-old when a Browns running back fumbled the ball on the 2-yard line, leading to the infamous drive by Denver's John Elway that snuffed Cleveland's only chance of playing in the Super Bowl. Now there he was body-slamming a Browns fan as a member of the hated Steelers. "I thought I was the biggest outlaw in Cleveland," said Porter to the media afterward, referring to the pre-game incident

In one of his many YouTube moments, Harrison leaps high over LaDainian Tomlinson, the Chargers star running back, after intercepting a Drew Brees pass in 2005.

with the Browns running back the previous year. He told Harrison, "If you get fined, the guys will chip in, because that was a laugh I'm going to remember forever." There was no fine.

While he did not get on the field much on the regular defense, Harrison excelled as a role player, accumulating eight special teams game balls that fill the shelves of his home office. During that time Parise said Omar Khan, the Steelers chief negotiator, told him team officials believed Harrison was the best wedge blaster – the guy who tosses his body at the middle of the pack of kick return blockers – he'd ever seen. In fact, while he is a two-time Pro Bowler, his special teams play is so extraordinary that the Steelers continue to use him in that role.

As Harrison watched from the sidelines, Porter piled up 10.5 sacks, two interceptions and a fumble recovery en route to a trip to the Pro Bowl. Haggans recorded nine sacks and 40 tackles, but once again was felled by injury late in the season, giving Harrison significant playing time during the final three games.

Harrison played well. The highlight was an interception of a Drew Brees pass against the San Diego Chargers – the same guy he knocked around at Purdue during a game with Kent – which he returned for 25 yards. His dramatic 3-foot-high leap over LaDainian Tomlinson, the Chargers star running back trying to tackle him on the return, made the weekly NFL highlight reels and remains a YouTube staple to this day.

The coaches were realizing the more they put him on the field, the more plays he made, especially as a rush linebacker whose job was to blow by or fight through offensive tackles to attack the quarterback. To do that, he used his short stature that NFL scouts scoffed at only a few years earlier to gain leverage on much bigger players. His unrelenting style made a difference in every game he entered. He showed an innate toughness that scouts didn't see when they turned up their noses at him.

"You're never going to hear me say that somebody is tougher than me, because I don't believe there is anyone," he says matter-of-factly, which is as close to braggadocio as Harrison gets.

While he had often caused his own problems or been thwarted by others, now he was adding a dose of maturity to his strong will, determination and focus to take advantage of opportunities he got due to others' misfortune. Harrison would never have gotten a chance to show what he could do if Jason Gildon and Clark Haggans hadn't come up lame in an exhibition game his rookie season.

Two years later, after being cut twice by the Steelers, he says, "it is guaranteed" that if Haggans had not broken his fingers in a weight-lifting injury he would not have gotten a final shot. And if not for Porter's boneheaded act before that Browns game, he might have never gotten a second, relatively early-career chance to show his coaches what he could do in a regular season game.

Then there was his successful three-game stretch during the Steelers 2005 Super Bowl season that was a result of another Haggans injury. With Haggans back for the playoffs, the Steelers dispensed with the top three teams in the playoffs (Cincinnati, Indianapolis and Denver) to become the first sixth-seed to earn a trip to the Super Bowl. In Detroit the Steelers won Super Bowl XL over Seattle by a score of 21-10, becoming one of only two teams to win the big game five times. Although Harrison was not a major factor on the defensive side of the ball, he earned his ring by making a team-high three special teams tackles.

While Harrison was elated and celebrated with his teammates, it was nothing like the 2009 victory. "I don't even consider it mine. I had a part in it, started a few games here and there, but I don't really consider that as a key part to the victory. It doesn't weigh as much in my mind as this one did," he said of the latest championship.

A few months later, no one noticed when Harrison passed on a chance to join the team for a trip to the White House and President George W. Bush. Two years later, his celebrity was such that he would create a national furor when he refused to participate in a White House visit with President Barack Obama.

14

Who Wants to be a Millionaire?

By the time Harrison was fitted for his first Super Bowl ring, he had not only proved himself as one of the best special teams player in the league, but also that he could play every position in the Steelers defense on a moment's notice. Most of all, the coaches realized what coaches dating back to Pee Wee football had found – Harrison made plays.

From his agent's perspective, he was also a supreme bargain, making only (by NFL standards) $286,000 a year. While his offer to renegotiate Harrison's deal had been rejected a year earlier, after the Super Bowl victory, Parise persuaded the team to reopen it with a year left. After carefully calculating the numbers Harrison put up, Parise showed Steelers officials that when Harrison played as a starter, he had a dominating influence on games. To him, that proved Harrison, despite the late career start, "was certainly going to be a star."

While the Steelers thought Parise was using stats to his advantage in the abstract, he argued they did not lie. Projected over 16 games, the number of tackles, interceptions and other plays the second-string linebacker made showed statistically "he was better than everyone around him," Parise said, including players who made the Pro Bowl. In fact, Parise argued, his stats proved that when he was on the field, he was among the top four or five players at his position in the league.

Of course, the Steelers pointed out Harrison wasn't on the field that often, but the fact that he was so good on special teams and was the first-line backup at every linebacker spot prompted them to seriously consider tearing up his old pact.

Another factor that helped Harrison was the predicament the team was in with Porter, one of his best friends on the team. Porter, who had just turned 30, had two years left on his back-loaded, multimillion dollar deal that was straining the Steelers position under the NFL salary cap. Because it included $5 million in roster bonuses for 2007 and more in 2008, Parise said it became clear during the negotiations on Harrison's new deal that Porter would be gone when his contract was over. It also became clear to Parise that "the Steelers wanted to guarantee they had stability at the position in the near future."

During the negotiations, Parise pressed the issue that they needed him on special teams and as the first guy off the bench at every linebacker position, which in the injury-riddled NFL is a valuable commodity. He was also keenly aware that the Steelers depth at linebacker – traditionally its strongest position – was so weak that the team would draft linebackers with their top picks just a few months later. "I told them he was going to be the guy who replaced Joey Porter," Parise said, even though he had no idea how soon that would be.

After prolonged but harmonious negotiations, Harrison agreed to a four-year, $6.4 million contract, which Parise characterized as the best deal in the league for a non-starter. "We went out and celebrated, and he was crazy happy. We were all immensely proud." Parise said it was the happiest he's seen Harrison, other than when his first child was born a few years later.

After years of professional uncertainty and many anxious moments since he left Kent, Harrison had found financial stability. "I would not have to worry about money again."

He bought an expansive and comfortable house in the North Hills and a couple of cars and trucks. He bought his dad and mom vehicles and fixed up their house. Instead of going on spending sprees, he started looking for conservative investments, hoping to make his money grow. "James pretty much tended to business and kept to the values he had," Parise said.

Parise built bonuses into the new deal that would add about $800,000 a year if Harrison played 50 percent of the snaps in the contract's final two years. But it could be argued that the Steelers got the better of the deal. What Parise and Harrison couldn't know was that the Steelers were going to cut Porter before the 2007 season.

So just a year after that momentous signing, James Harrison became a starter, turning the best contract ever for a non-starter into a great deal for the Steelers, who now had a starting linebacker for three years at a discount.

"I went from having the best contract in the league for a non-starter to the best bargain for a team in the NFL in one summer," he said.

15

Sticking to Success

Coming off the first Super Bowl victory in 25 years, the team was in a state of flux. They lost several players to free agency, and then things got worse when the quarterback was almost killed in a motorcycle crash near Downtown Pittsburgh. When he miraculously recovered from face and body injuries that could have been much worse, Roethlisberger was knocked out again with an appendectomy just before the season began.

The Steelers, however dipped to a 4-7 record after eleven games, but fought back to an 8-8 record. Harrison continued to labor away on special teams, credited with 15 tackles, including a game high four against Jacksonville. He suffered a high ankle sprain against San Diego, which rendered him inactive for six weeks. He replaced Haggans for his only start of the season in the last game against Cincinnati. He had three solo tackles and was credited for hurrying the quarterback once.

Shortly after the season's end, Cowher retired from the Steelers, making way for Mike Tomlin, the first black head coach ever hired by the Steelers, who came aboard on Jan. 22, 2007.

Two months later, just a week before a $1 million roster bonus would kick in, followed by $4 million more before training camp, Porter was released, only to sign a bigger deal with the Miami Dolphins. Steelers officials called it a "business decision" based on the NFL salary cap, when, in fact, they decided to shed Porter for the unheralded free agent, who just two years earlier none of the 32 NFL teams wanted.

LeBeau, who was a big fan of Porter, said his unit remained among the best in the league. "I don't expect us to miss a beat with James Harrison in there at the outside backer," he said during a 2007 mini-camp. "Any games that he's played, our defense has not missed a beat and he's always been a contributing factor to that, so I have every confidence in the world in him."

James Farrior, the veritable quarterback of the defense at inside linebacker, also chimed in. "He's not Joey Porter," Farrior told the media, "but he's a great player. We're not expecting any kind of drop off. He's going to do good things out there."

The new coach also had a positive spin: "I have an idea of what I think James Harrison is capable of, and I think it's going to be more than enough," said Tomlin. "We're going to get great outside linebacker play."

Despite those protestations, just months later the Steelers used their first two draft picks on linebackers – Lawrence Timmons of Florida State and LaMarr Woodley of Michigan. Parise said it was not a reflection on Harrison but on the team's need to replenish its linebacker corps.

Harrison quickly showed that the confidence his coaches and teammates had in him was not misplaced, having the breakout year his agent projected during contract negotiations. During a 38-7 humiliation of the Ravens on "Monday Night Football" in November 2007, Harrison not only forced three fumbles, piled up 2.5 sacks, intercepted a pass and recovered a fumble – in the first half – but went on to finish with 3.5 sacks and nine tackles. Six times, he hurried the quarterback. All this, against the team that had cut him four years earlier.

If that weren't enough, Harrison made another enduring You-Tube moment against Baltimore when he put a thunderous hit on Ed Reed during a punt return that no doubt left the defensive back wondering where he was. While his teammates gloried in his accomplishments on the league's biggest regular-season stage, he said he had nothing to brag about when the network interviewers approached. "No way. I just happened to have a good day."

He continued to draw more notice on his way to his first Pro Bowl. His dominating play on national television prompted network announcers to call him "Mr. Monday Night." Harrison doesn't like that tag because he considers himself a player who expends all of his energy on every play, no matter the day of the week, although he will admit to enjoying the big games, especially in Pittsburgh "with the city into it and the crowds and all."

Other nicknames have been attached to Harrison. His friends on the team have called him "Debo" for his menacing appearance that resembled the character in the inner-city stoner movie "Friday." The oldest is "Silverback," given to him by Porter and former defensive back Dwayne Washington. They admired the way Harrison "de-cleated" or knocked much larger opponents off their feet with power resembling the silverback gorilla, said to be 27 times stronger than man. It has been picked up by the media to the point that he has been offered business opportunities capitalizing on it, which he has so far declined. While the nickname could be construed as having racist overtones, Harrison likes it: "It depends how it's used. Now if you call me a gorilla..."

His play was dominant during the 2007 season – 8.5 sacks, seven forced fumbles, three of them recovered, and 98 tackles – he was named the AFC Player of the Month for November and he recorded his first playoff sack in a losing effort against Jacksonville. His play was so dominating that his teammates voted him Most Valuable Player over Roethlisberger, both of whom made their first trips to the Pro Bowl. Grateful about the honor, he clearly values the opinion of his teammates over anyone else's.

"MVP of my own team means my teammates voted to say I deserve this honor, even though I don't look at myself in that good a light," he said with characteristic humility. He voted for Roethlisberger.

While he only rides in airplanes when he has to, he reluctantly made the trip to Hawaii for the Pro Bowl. He soon learned to be wary of some veteran All-Pros, because of their penchant for finding room numbers of the first-year all-stars and charging meals and other amenities to their rooms. The bills were often in the thousands of dollars, he was told. Harrison, who watches his money closely, was ready. He choose to eat most meals in his room, avoiding the hotel restaurants because of the pranksters. "I also made sure to never tell anyone my room number," he said.

Parise, his wife, Harrison's parents and other family members attended the week long festivities. On the practice field, Harrison did not know what to make of game preparations. Having never watched a Pro Bowl, Harrison approached it like any other football game he had played in. No nonsense. All business. "After one practice, he told me this wasn't football," Parise said.

Apparently, during practice, he didn't jog through plays like everyone else, causing the other players to ask him to calm down. "What do you mean? It's football," he said. Eventually, everyone convinced him that the game wasn't like the regular season, more of a pitch-and-catch exhibition for skill players. "It isn't a real game, there's no blitzing, no bump coverage, nothing like the real deal," he said.

During the actual game on a hot Hawaii day, Harrison found out what it was really all about. While he was happy to get extensive playing time at the outset, it had been weeks since he played a game, so he suffered in the heat. He noticed that whenever anyone wanted out of the game, they would raise a hand toward the bench for a replacement. When Harrison did that, no one came in, leaving him on the field for almost every play to the point of exhaustion, which his teammates considered great fun because of his attitude earlier in the week.

Harrison remembers waving at numerous defensive players during the game to spell him. When none of them reacted, Harrison simply took himself out for a play, leaving his team with only 10 defenders, but no one seemed to notice.

The comedic highlight for him was the way Steelers All-Pro Casey Hampton, the massive nose tackle, reacted to being placed on special teams. The 350-pound-plus behemoth asked off, but his request was refused. That's when he told the coaches, "I'll play it, but I ain't blocking," Harrison said. He will never forget Hampton standing on the field during the plays. "He never moved, didn't touch a soul," his teammate laughs.

16

The Best
of What's Around

A grueling off-season of workouts – some three times a day
– brought Harrison into 2008 camp in the best shape of
his life. From the start of the season, he was throwing
around much larger people as if they were mannequins.

He changed the course of the game in a win against the Ravens. He recorded a thunderous sack on Jacksonville's quarterback to preserve a win with just over a minute to play. It was another sack in that game in which he was flagged for unnecessary roughness that got him in trouble. Asked after the game about the play, a smiling Harrison said: "Ridiculous. You don't make a call like that unless (the official) might have money on it."

A few days later, the league levied a $20,000 fine on Harrison, which he appealed. Parise was his spokesman at the appeal. He initially tried to plead that the reporters got the nuances of Harrison's statement wrong. "That's when they clicked on a video, showing the interview," Parise said. On second thought, he tried to argue that Harrison was joking. "That didn't work either," Parise said, so Harrison paid the fine.

Harrison has had more than $50,000 taken out of his paychecks in fines over the years, the latest coming when he tackled Arizona Quarterback Matt Leinart in the Steelers opening exhibition game in August 2009. His $7,500 fine was for driving the quarterback into the ground, which Harrison denies. "It seems like you have to take a class on how to hit a quarterback nowadays," he said.

He also questions a new rule named after his teammate Hines Ward regarding crack back blocks. In the past, an offensive blocker was allowed to hit a defensive person however they wanted, but after Ward repeatedly knocked players out of games with thunderous blocks, the NFL instituted a new rule that prohibits hits from the shoulders up.

To Harrison, who is on the receiving end of such blocks, that makes no sense. "That is the craziest thing I've ever heard. You can't hit a guy from the shoulder up, but you can crack back on a guy below the waist, which could cut his knees and end his career?" Harrison said.

He prefers the old rules. "I'd rather a guy knock me silly and put me out for a game or two instead of ending my career with a knee injury with a below-the-waist block," he said.

Harrison did suffer what would be a debilitating injury for most players in the last preseason game of 2008, a separated joint in his shoulder, which limited his ability to lift his right arm. Instead of taking time off, Harrison received injections every week to allow him to play through the pain, even if it meant a day after of excruciating pain that reduced his range of motion on that side of his body to nil. He also was forced to take injections a year earlier when he suffered a hip injury that he still does not have a clear diagnosis on. He said the shoulder injury forced him to take more time than usual during the past off-season to let it heal. He says it is fine now.

Unlike other Pro Bowl players, Harrison continued to play special teams, which produced one of the most comical – except for Steeler fans -- plays of the season. In week eight against the reigning Super Bowl champs, the New York Giants, Greg Warren, the Steelers long snapper, suffered a season-ending knee injury earlier in the game.

In the fourth quarter, with the Steelers clinging to a 14-12 lead and punting from their own end zone, Harrison was sent in as the long snapper. It was the first time he'd ever served in that role. He promptly hiked the ball well over punter Mitch Berger's head for a safety, which tied the score. The excellent field position after the free kick allowed the Giants to march down the field for the game winning touchdown with about three minutes to go. The 21-14 loss dropped the Steelers to a 5-2 record.

Months later, when asked about the play: "What did I do? I hiked the ****** ****** over his head," he said. He said Far-rior told him he could've done it, which prompted Harrison to tell him, "Then you get your butt out there the next time."

But that miscue would be the exception. Over the next few weeks, he created mayhem against San Diego with sacks and interceptions, including another YouTube moment when Harrison made an acrobatic, over-the-head interception, then leaped over a Charger defender as he galloped 33-yards down the field, set-ting the Steelers up for a touchdown.

Harrison made critical sacks against the New England Patriots and much more, leading his teammates to vote him their best player and earning a second consecutive selection to the Pro Bowl. His efforts and those of his teammates led the Steelers to a 12-4 record, their second consecutive AFC North Division championship after beating the Ravens in Baltimore in Week 15, giving them an AFC-best 19 division titles. Harrison sat out with a hip injury so he could get healthy for the playoffs as the team lost to Tennessee and beat Cleveland to end the campaign.

He had a career high 16 sacks, breaking a club record set by Mike Merriweather in 1984. He led the NFL with seven forced fumbles. The dynamic duo of Harrison and Woodley piled up 27.5 sacks, breaking a team record set in 1994 by Kevin Greene and Greg Lloyd. Finally, he cemented his position as the best linebacker in the league when he was voted Associated Press De-fensive Player of the Year, leaving DeMarcus Ware of the Dallas Cowboys 50 points behind.

That didn't change Harrison's opinion of himself. During a press conference celebrating the honor, a reporter pointed out that leg-ends such as Joe Greene, Mel Blount, Rod Woodson and Jack Lam-bert were the only other Steelers so honored. Since all of them are in the Pro Football Hall of Fame, Harrison was asked if he thought he belongs in the same company. "No," he said. To be considered in that company, he'd have to perform at a high level for many

years to come, just as those before him had done. When pressed
about his success, he credited not his enormous reserves of perse-
verance and will but his teammates and coaches such as LeBeau.

Then, typical of his honest self-appraisal, he said his success
might have to do with his relatively short stature – less than
6-feet tall – and the reaction massive offensive lineman have to
it. "It could be leverage, strength or just the fact that they're
taller than me and can't bend down that low to get to me. Guys
also might figure they got a little dude here and might just be
overlooking me," he said in mock indignation. "As far as the way
I feel, I think of myself as an average player who has experienced some success. I guess I have a hard time patting myself
on the back because one minute they say you're the greatest
thing walking and the next minute they're going to tell you to go
ahead and give up the game because it's not working for you."

Harrison won a long list of other prestigious honors in 2008.
He was named Defensive Player of the Year by the NFL Alumni,
an award voted upon by pro football retirees who played the
same positions as the honorees. He was up for three ESPYs from
ESPN for spectacular plays, was named AFC Player of the Week,
as well as similar honors from league sponsor General Motors.
Perhaps the most esteemed honor ever bestowed on Harrison
came on the eve of the 2009 season when he was named a team
captain. He said he accomplished all the things he has by using
a singular focus that rivals anyone in sports or in any other walk
of life.

He figures if he does what he is supposed to do in preparation
and in games, it does not matter who is on the field. The actions
of opponents are not his concerns, unless someone like Arizona's
Aaron Francisco tries to cut his knees. In fact, he maintains such
a detached view of the opposition that he often doesn't even
know their names. "I couldn't even tell you right now the name
of the guy I played against in the Super Bowl. I know their numbers, but I can't see past the jersey. I just look at the number."

17

The Largest
Contract Ever

Just three years into his four-year deal, it was clear that Harrison, who had reached his 30th birthday, was now a bargain by any conceivable NFL standard. Harrison knew it. Parise knew it. So did the rest of the NFL players.

Shortly after they arrived in Hawaii for his second Pro Bowl, virtually every all-star he met approached Parise with some friendly advice. "They hugged me, they mugged me, telling me to get their 'man' his money, which was an indication they really cared about James," Parise said. As usual, Harrison maintained a stoic attitude but was mindful of what he thought was his due. "I've done everything I'm supposed to do," he said of his dominance on the field and accolades that earned him the right to get paid with the best. Looking over the contracts of other linebackers who earned two or three times his salary, he casually insisted he had reached that point, too. "This is where I'm supposed to be," he said of a new, monstrous contract that would set him up for life.

Parise got right on it. He called Steelers negotiator Omar Khan from Hawaii at 10 p.m. Pittsburgh time to start the dialogue. After they returned, the talks developed well with the low-key Khan, who Parise praises as one of the best in the business. The two sat down at the NFL Scouting Combine in Indianapolis to set the parameters of what Harrison was worth to see if they could come to terms, or if Harrison would simply play out the final year of his contract for $2.1 million and test the free agent market.

Once again, Parise said the numbers Harrison had amassed set him apart from most, if not all, of his peers. While Harrison had successfully shed the baggage he brought with him to the NFL, Parise realized he was facing the Steelers with a smallish guy who was 30 years old – late middle age by NFL standards – and that the Steelers had let linebackers such as Porter, Haggans and others go when they got to that age and were set to make huge bucks.

"My job was to make a logical, analytical approach to the contract," Parise said. "Emotion and posturing wouldn't get it done," he said of the negotiations that got scant mention in the newspapers. While Parise was keeping it low-key, Harrison was not during his daily discussions with the agent. He was keenly aware of what other defensive players made. As negotiations heated up, Tennessee's Albert Haynesworth, a defensive lineman, signed a free-agent deal with the Washington Redskins that was said to be worth $100 million. The Steelers hadn't offered even half that much. "I didn't want more than him," Harrison said. "I just wanted to be paid for what I'd done."

As Parise developed the deal, Harrison was becoming agitated. He knew this contract was the one that could secure his future. At his age, he also knew it was his one chance to get the big bucks. He realized he was in a perfect situation with LeBeau and the Steelers, so he wasn't against a hometown discount. But he was not about to take less than half of what Haynesworth got.

Eventually Parise convinced Harrison that Haynesworth's contract – like many others in the NFL – was not what it seemed. "It was a charade," Parise said. While the total package for Hayne-sworth was $100 million, only about $45 million of it was obtain-able up front. Parise said more than half of the Haynesworth deal is to be paid at the end of his contract. Because of the way that contract and others – like Joey Porter's – are back-loaded, most of them get cut before they ever see the money. That is why in the current NFL culture, the amount of cash players get up front in signing bonuses is key.

While Harrison never personally entered into the negotiations, he had plenty to say to Parise during the process. As the Steel-ers hit him with what he considered one low-ball offer after an-other, Harrison would tell his agent to walk away if the team didn't bring the offer up to at least the top five salary brackets for linebackers. It was pure business, Harrison said.

It was a prickly period of time between agent and player, but none of it leaked out. Looking back, Parise smiles and says: "James will bait you. He's good at baiting you. You never know for sure what he's doing." While Harrison was emphatically stat-ing his position to Parise on a daily, if not hourly basis, the pro-cess with the Steelers moved on methodically and calmly. Parise said, "There were a few times when I felt like it would fail at any minute, but that never happened. That's because the Steelers always made it clear they wanted him."

While Harrison had dispelled decisively the size, speed and at-titude marks against him earlier in his career, now the only nega-tive was his age, which would be 31 at the start of the 2009 sea-son. Parise would argue that that was a non-issue. "The guy has no mileage on him," he said. "I argued he's like buying a 2000 car with only 2,000 miles on it. It's new."

Because Parise and Harrison are certain that his workout regi-men means he can play into his late 30s, the agent was decided-ly against that back-loading of the contract that portends a quick exit when the big numbers come due. They wanted to make sure the new contract was structured in a way that Harrison had a chance of getting all of it.

"The majority of his money was going to be up front and in the first three years, not like a lot of these other crap contracts," Parise said. It was during the Pirates home opener when Ed Bouchette, the Post-Gazette's Steelers beat writer, broke the story from a bar next to PNC Park where he was doing a radio show: The Steelers had signed Harrison to the largest contract in NFL history for a linebacker. He received $13 million up front in a six-year $52 million contract, which was also the largest sum the team ever promised to a defensive player. He'd receive $20 million guaranteed and $26 million in the first three years of the deal, which means he'd make about $200,000 a game.

At a press conference the next day, team president Art Rooney II stated: "Over the last several years, James has demonstrated time and again that hard work and persistence pays off." Harrison, decked out in a custom-made suit, thanked God and the Steelers, in that order. The first question, from Bouchette, was whether Harrison had spent more money on the threads than the $4,000 he got in bonus money for his first free agent contract.

After acknowledging it was close, he allowed the laughter to die down before talking about what the contract means. "I want to be a Steeler for life. It's great to be here. I am with the best team in the league." He said he had not reached his peak and with hard work he knows he can get better. "I'll just be a little more reckless on the field. I don't have to worry about too much anymore. I can get back to doing what I do best." As for the money, he said the sheer enormity of it hadn't sunk in yet, but that he knew "it's a lot."

As everyone knew about his fear of flying, a smiling Harrison joked that the contract would have been finished weeks earlier if Steelers brass had conceded to his demand that he get the chance to fly in a plane piloted by Steelers Chairman Dan Rooney. Four years earlier, Rooney was involved in a highly publicized crash in his personal plane en route from Pittsburgh to the team's training camp in Latrobe. Sitting in the back of the room, Rooney laughed heartily.

The Bill Parise family enjoying themselves in Hawaii

Harrison also said the first person he called after the deal was done was his mother. Her first question: "How much?" he said with a laugh. He'd already bought his parents new cars and other nice things, but now he is building them a dream house in Akron. At the end of the conference, Harrison said simply it was time to go back to work.

18

The Gold Standard in the Gym

Parise knows a thing or two about getting in shape. A picture of him performing the Olympic Cross at the University of New Mexico, a brutally difficult gymnastic maneuver on hanging rings where one arm extends out 45 degrees, the other straight back, adorns the wall of his Beaver County YMCA office.

After a stellar career as a college gymnast, he coached gymnastics near his alma mater, then returned to Western Pennsylvania to begin careers in business and managing YMCAs, all the while promoting physical fitness. He has been a personal trainer, which led to a career as a sports agent in the 1980s. He has represented, among many others, Roger Kingdom, the two-time Olympic gold medalist hurdler from the University of Pittsburgh, and Mike Webster, the late Steeler Hall of Fame center. He also has mentored Olympic silver medalist Lauryn Williams of Rochester, Pa., who anchored a 4x100 high school relay team, which included Parise's daughter Devin, and won the Pennsylvania state championship. Williams is a hopeful for the 2010 Olympics.

He devised strength and speed training regimens for all his athletes, including working with Harrison during the early days as his agent. When Parise went to work for Harrison, he already knew from watching tape that he was a dynamic football player, but he didn't realize why. "The first time I met him, it was clear he was a (workout) freak," Parise said. He had a tremendous physique. Parise said he also showed the kind of strength he had never seen. "I remember giving him a bench press workout one day and he was so far ahead of everyone else that it was ridiculous."

Harrison today uses virtually every legal method he can find to give him an edge, including regular treatments by a masseuse and acupuncture. He spends time in a hyperbaric oxygen chamber in his dining room, which is supposed to replenish his blood oxygen levels to help him heal more quickly. His demeanor and body mass have led some to believe Harrison was using performance-enhancing drugs, a subject Parise has learned much about as an agent over the past 25 years.

He quickly realized Harrison had none of the traits associated with the practice. His body wasn't scarred with the acne that plagues steroid users. His muscularity was not unevenly distributed. His head had not grown. As he got to know him, he realized another thing about Harrison when it came to performance-enhancing drugs: "James would view that as a shortcut, and James doesn't take shortcuts," he said. "He's hard-wired to do it the right way, and there is no compromise."

Steroids? Human growth hormones? "Test me any time you want." Harrison says. "Like my dad said about gangs, steroids are for punks and pussies. I have never taken a steroid or injected myself with HGH or anything like that. Everything I have is from hard work and dedication. It is not a fluke. I put the work in to get the result I've gotten."

One of the reasons for these intense workouts is his reality-based notion of his job.

"The way I see it is, I have a short period of time to make a whole lot of money to set myself up for life. In that time frame, I'm going to try to get as many years in as I can. The more I practice, work out and make myself better, the longer I'm going to have in the league. I'll take the five to 10 years or whatever it might be of not going on vacation and not doing this and that so I can set myself up to do whatever I want to do when I'm done, or go wherever I want to go," he said.

One thing Parise found in the early going was that Harrison's running style was out of whack, slowing him down. An expert on running form through his work with track athletes, Parise noticed it the first time Harrison ran a 40-yard dash. "He could run a 4.8 in the 40 (adequate but not fast by NFL linebacker standards), but he had terrible form," Parise said. "His feet went out making him run like a duck."

The agent realized how focused Harrison was about his craft when he quickly embraced a new running style and dropped his time by .2 of a second in a matter of days. "That's why he blows people up (on the field)," Parise said, dispelling the myth that his client wasn't fast enough for the NFL. (Harrison said he hasn't been timed in the 40 since he made the Steelers and doesn't know how fast he is.)

What impressed Parise more than anything was the work ethic Harrison exhibited from the day they met. "I've never represented an athlete who works harder, and I've worked with great athletes and Olympic gold medalists," he said.

Mike Webster was known for pushing blocking sleds 50 yards at a time and running laps and laps up and down the steep upper deck at Three Rivers Stadium that earned him the reputation as one of the toughest, hardest working professional football players ever. Parise says Harrison works harder. "James is clearly more focused on things that improve him as a player," he said. "I think he clearly understands how strong he is, but it (his work ethic) instills confidence in him because he feels he's outworked everyone else," Parise said.

Harrison never stops either. Knowing that athletes need down time to allow muscles to repair themselves, Parise early on pleaded in vain with Harrison to take time off. "The only reason he didn't work out the day after the (2009) Super Bowl was because he was traveling," Parise said. "He was going to take a couple of days off after that but hit the weight room the next day." The off-season workouts sometimes number as many as three a day.

Over the past few years, Parise has given way to another personal trainer who feels the same way about Harrison. Steve Saunders of the Power Train Institute of Lancaster, Pa., met Harrison about five years ago through Dan Krieder, a once-undersized Steelers fullback who built his body into an extremely powerful mass through the PTI program that focuses on intensive speed and strength improvement. When Harrison saw the results, he asked Kreider for an introduction. Saunders, a four-year starter, captain and all-league performer in football at Millersville University, has worked with more than 100 professional athletes.

He recently also opened gyms in Pittsburgh and Philadelphia. Along with Harrison, Saunders has helped Steelers Chris Kemoeatu, Willie Colon, Hines Ward, Heath Miller, Matt Spaeth and others. His program has helped Paul Posluszny of Hopewell, Penn State and now the Buffalo Bills build a massive body. In just four months, his regimen enabled Aaron Maybin of Penn State to gain 20 pounds of muscle, enough to make him a first-round draft choice of the Buffalo Bills. Many others have also benefited from the unique training regimen that focuses on helping players develop quick bursts of speed and football strength – the ability to handle massive forces in brief spurts.

Harrison is not only his greatest success, but his massive body is featured on the front page of Saunders' Web site (www.powertrainsports.com). Knowing that even the most conditioned athletes have weaknesses, he was still impressed with Harrison from the day they met. "He was relatively fit, and fast in certain movements, but my goal from the outset was to make the entire package stronger and faster," Saunders said.

Harrison's biggest initial attribute was his genetics. He had a compact body, good muscle tone, but most of all, "once we found things that could be improved, Harrison's attitude was that he

James Sr. Proudly stands with his son after being named Associated Press Defensive Player of the Year.

would do whatever was necessary to see how strong and fast he could get," his trainer said.

Like just about everyone the player encounters, Saunders said Harrison was reserved when they met. But after the grueling regimen began, Harrison "came out of his shell pretty fast" and the duo started building an enduring friendship that is laced with non-stop banter. "He and I have a pretty unique relationship where we constantly break each other's balls. I found he likes someone who can stand his ground against him," he said.

Along with intensive workouts, Saunders builds diet and nutritional supplement programs for everyone he works with. In Harrison's case, it is a low-carbohydrate, high-protein diet. Harrison said if he didn't watch his intake of carbs, he would have no trouble piling 25 more pounds on his 250-pound body. "I wouldn't consider him a really strict diet person, but he still gets it and follows it for the most part, even if he does occasionally stray," Saunders said.

The bottom line is that Harrison has built an incredible muscle mass that keeps making him stronger and faster, and at age 31, he has not peaked. "He keeps getting better and better because when you work like James does, if he is lucky enough to avoid a freak injury and keeps taking care of himself, I don't think he's going to be at his best until his mid-30s," Saunders said, echoing what LeBeau and Parise have argued.

"Shoot, he's got a lot of miles left in that engine. He's stronger and faster right now than he's ever been. That big contract didn't change his work ethic, other than make him work harder this year than he ever has," Saunders said. He sets the bar high, too. Only one person has won the Defensive MVP award twice in a row – Lawrence Taylor, the New York Giants Hall of Famer. Harrison would like to be the second one.

Just as on the football field, Harrison can do things in the weight room that astonish some of the strongest men there. "For a 250-pound guy, he can outlift any lineman on that team and he can run with about any wide receiver," Saunders said. As for Harrison's football speed, during off-season workouts, he has watched the hulking linebacker run stride-for-stride with former Steeler, now Redskin Antwaan Randle El, one of the speediest receivers in the league.

Harrison is one of Saunders' favorites in the workout room, but he admits he has to ready himself for the "mental joust." "He'll show up and act like he doesn't want to work until I start breaking his stones," Saunders said. In lightning-quick responses, Harrison returns the favor with insults about Saunders age, race and thinning hair as the strenuous workouts move along. When Harrison picks on him, Saunders starts taunting him about his size and conditioning. Then it degenerates into a good-natured fight over who is taller. During one workout, Saunders, who stands 6-feet tall, ventured up to a full-length mirror next to Harrison and said, "See, I'm taller." Harrison disputed that before they get into a childish stare down, neither relenting before it was time for the next exercise.

The no-holds-barred byplay can get revved up. Last spring, after Harrison had aimed some barbs at Saunders, the trainer pulled up the football player's shirt and asked him if he's seen any abdominal muscles lately, calling the muscular Harrison "soft." Harrison showed him his taut stomach, marveling, "Yeah, man, look at those abs."

As Harrison painfully hoisted barbells, Saunders called a cadence of start and stop motions and laughed at the football player's struggle. "Look at how he backs off the last rep," Saunders said as Harrison grunted through yet another brutal arm exercise. "I'll bet others in the league do all of them."

"You told me the range is 8-10. I did 8," Harrison responds. "I said 10," Saunders laughed. Harrison came back with an insult about his trainer's family tree.

They also talk about life and football and on one day, about complaints Harrison had about the massive contract he would soon sign. "Take the money, James," Saunders told him. "Where are you going to enjoy the same quality of work and life you have here?" As the complaining Harrison pressed on, the trainer scoffed. "Before he made money, he was a lot less difficult."

"That's because he makes these exercises up as we go along," Harrison said after doing a particularly difficult arm curl in which he slowly brought a barbell up to his chest, then rolled the weights over in the middle of a lift to strain his bulging arms, making brief stops every six inches or so to increase muscle strain and mass. As Saunders prodded him through the complicated exercises, correcting him every time he's more than an inch or so off, or a fraction of a second too quick, Harrison shoots back, "Let me see you do this," which causes his well-built trainer to laugh heartily.

On this day, the workout was at the Robert Morris University facility at Neville Island, where Harrison's impressive performance caused most to stop and watch Harrison move from drill to drill with only minutes in between. The taunting never ceases – probably because it's a way to divert Harrison's attention from the demanding program. At one point after Harrison's incessant complaints, Saunders told a bystander he was opening a new facility in Pittsburgh's North Hills. Harrison mockingly suggested he was going to do the same thing. "I'm going to open the James Harrison gym right next door, and then we'll see who can do business," Harrison laughed.

During a more serious moment, Saunders says the program Harrison follows is one of the most intense to be found. "It is literally a case of 'don't try this at home,' " Saunders said. They are broken down into four categories where a different part of his body is the subject of each workout for his torso, his arms, his middle body core and legs. There are strenuous barbell shoulder presses and complicated bar curls where he slowly rolls a heavy dumbbell as his trainer counts off a cadence. That torso workout ends with dumbbell strength exercises on a declining board and other things called "spider curls" and a "Barbell Cuban press."

Harrison's arms didn't grow wide and large by accident. In the rigors of that workout, he is contorted in several incline and decline positions as he labors through arm exercises that would render most of us paralyzed after one repetition. The leg workout is even more intense with exercise after exercise including step-ups with heavy weights in his hands and hip, ankle and other strenuous sets. "If anyone tried to go out and do it, it would blow them away to see how far ahead he is," Saunders said.

The price Harrison pays in his workouts will increase the longevity of his career. "The program builds on itself. He's performing better. He's healthier, stronger, faster," Saunders said.

The one additional factor that has catapulted Harrison: his will to succeed.

19

Mean or Shy?

From childhood on, almost everyone first encountering Harrison met a foreboding, even menacing-looking person who gave the impression he'd just as soon smack you as look at you. You felt he could snap at any minute. In reality, the few he lets get close soon learn that the fearsome persona is merely a steely façade to keep people away.

He was and still is extremely shy. Harrison is so terrified about speaking in front of large audiences that the experience can make him sick. He'll whack a quarterback in front of 65,000 at Heinz Field, but if he has to talk before a much smaller crowd, he freaks out. Parise has fielded hundreds of requests for speaking engagements – many for big money – but Harrison has spurned almost all of them.

In fact, when asked who Harrison has turned down, Parise says "everyone," which includes an impressive list of talk shows, sports programs and prestigious events. The problem is not only his reticence, but his fear of flying as well. He'd rather stay home than sweat through an hour or two on an airplane. The recent rash of plane crashes – which Harrison pays close attention to – doesn't help.

But sometimes he has to relent. Speaking invitations have multiplied now that he is the defensive MVP of the NFL. But that doesn't mean he feels any better about it. That mystifies Parise and others who have watched Harrison in front of crowds. When coaxed into appearances, or if he must face the hot lights of the media – as he had to when he signed the new big contract in early 2009 – he almost always delivers cordial, friendly and thoughtful remarks.

There is no better example of his acute introversion than the annual banquet of the NFL Alumni Association, which chose him as defensive player of the year. Harrison was invited to the $10,000-a-table event at the Hyatt Regency of Tampa two days before the 2009 Super Bowl to receive a crystal vase. At least he was already in town for the game, so he didn't have to get on another airplane.

Those on hand included NFL Hall of Famers and glitzy celebrities and stars in town for the NFL's greatest weekend. Dressed in his finest suit, Harrison became extremely nervous when lights flashed and a music intro blared as Merril Hoge, former Steelers running back and now ESPN commentator, took the stage to emcee. The alumni association honors are especially gratifying because the members of the group – all former NFL Players – do the voting. What's more, they can vote only on guys who played their position. In every instance, a Hall of Famer at that position presents the award.

Things seemed fine as Parise and Harrison were spirited into a limousine for the short trip to the hotel. Because Harrison was so focused on the upcoming game, the dutiful agent had punched in a few notes in his Blackberry for Harrison's speech before he left his room. Harrison briefly looked at the notes and told Parise he didn't need them. As they moved through the crowd to their seats, Parise noticed something was wrong with Harrison. "I'm outta here, Bill," he said, his bald head beaded with sweat. "I ain't going up there."

With almost six years as his agent, Parise was well aware of

Harrison during a moment of reflection after receiving
his Super Bowl XLIII ring.

Harrison's aversion to public speaking, so he simply told him to
calm down, do a quick thank-you and go back to the team hotel.
That wasn't going to work, Harrison said. He was going to slip
out and asked Parise to tell the sponsors he had an 8 p.m. team
meeting he couldn't miss. His agent told him he wasn't going to
do that either.

Parise thought Harrison had overcome his anxiety by the time
a steward arrived to escort him backstage. Then a few minutes
later the steward returned to say Harrison wanted him. "I told
her I was not coming back there. I had no reason to. She said,
'I think he's going to get sick. I think he's going to pass out. You
need to come,' " said Parise.

By the time he got backstage, Harrison was sweating profusely,
looking peaked and immovable as he stood awaiting his call to
the stage.

Harrison: "Bill, I ain't doing this. You do it." Parise: "They want to hear you, not me.'"

As a video clip of Harrison on the football field began to roll, he didn't budge. Finally, Parise said he'd go out with him. As Parise held the curtain, Harrison relented and walked into the bright lights to greet Hall of Fame Linebacker Bobby Bell of the Kansas City Chiefs, the presenter.

Instead of following him, Parise stopped in his tracks, leaving his client on his own.

Harrison wasn't happy with the trick but went ahead to accept the award with grace and charm and without notes. "Oh my God, he was wonderful. He was just absolutely wonderful," Parise said, calling it "a real growing experience" for Harrison.

Not that Harrison is now comfortable under the lights. In fact, whether it is the press conference over his new contract or interviews on national television, Harrison still complains of nervousness, while coming off as cool and self-assured.

He remains extremely reluctant. While his teammates do TV shows, commercials and public appearances during the season, Harrison – who does some charitable work in the off-season –does almost nothing.

It's not as if he hasn't given it a try. After the 2009 Super Bowl, Parise said Harrison wanted to capitalize on his new stardom by making appearances, doing autograph shows and other events that could earn him as much as a quarter of a million dollars. But only a few weeks into events that drew huge throngs, Harrison begged off.

"He just could not stand being in those crowds with all those people," Parise said. "That's because he's basically a shy guy."

20

The Politics of Football

In 2005, when the Steelers won their fifth Super Bowl, Harrison was a relatively unknown special teams player few outside Steeler Nation had ever heard of. So when he didn't accompany the team to the White House for a congratulatory visit with President George W. Bush, no one noticed. Harrison, who says he's for any politician that can help "me keep my money" from the tax man, had no intention of going to the White House in 2009 either, even with the first black president in office.

What he did not understand was that he was no longer that obscure special teamer. As the reigning NFL Defensive Player of the Year who executed the longest play in Super Bowl history, every public move was now an event. He would soon find that if he became embroiled in controversy, the whole world was watching.

Even in the crazed domain of Steeler Nation where 10,000 people show up for summer practices, Harrison had never felt the scrutiny he would face just before the team's trip to Washington D.C. A week earlier, Harrison was at a charity golf event – he doesn't play golf but went to support a teammate – when a reporter from WTAE-TV in Pittsburgh asked him if he was looking forward to meeting the president. Harrison jokingly said he didn't go before, and he wasn't going this time either. According to Harrison's logic, he didn't like his team being singled out just because they won.

"If you want to see the Pittsburgh Steelers, invite us when we don't win the Super Bowl," was his message to the president. "I don't feel the need to actually go," he said, lightheartedly suggesting he'd join his teammates in six years in an off-year after they've won "10 or 11 rings." The reality was that he just doesn't fly unless he has to, and this was not one of those occasions.

He quickly found that his new renown had turned a relatively innocuous attempt at a joke into a firestorm. The Pittsburgh media led the way, playing the story big from every conceivable angle. Then the video interview went viral on the Internet. Within days, the story was everywhere. The Obama snub was the subject on 419,000 Web postings. It was picked up by media around the world, including The New York Times, The Microsoft Network, The Huffington Post and ESPN.

Did he dislike the first black president? Was it fear of flying? Would he appear to be a racist if he snubbed the white president and not the black one? Wasn't this an insult to Dan Rooney, who supported Obama and was being considered for the ambassadorship to Ireland he would receive a few months later? Didn't he owe it to President Obama for supporting the Steelers in the Super Bowl?

Harrison said they all missed his point. "When it came down to it, I didn't want to go. The media made a big deal out of it because I'm a black person, and it's a black president. I had no desire to go to see the president, black, white, Puerto Rican, Chinese, whatever."

Harrison even had dustups with his own parents over the snub. Parise, who fielded more than 100 calls about the decision, characterized the entire event as ridiculous. "It was a suicidal mission he could not win," Parise said. A fear of flying was one thing, but the bottom line, according to his agent, was: "He did not want to go, and he didn't go. That's it."

What it would show Harrison once and for all is that now that he is a national star, every move he makes is subject to scrutiny. While Harrison and his agent thought the White House debacle was a non-event, that did not prevent Internet ranters from having a field day. If that wasn't enough publicity for an entire summer, a near-tragic event just a few days later put him back in the news.

21

The Most Important Things in Life

Harrison accepts his new-found celebrity and realizes how fleeting it will be. Now that he's a star, he feels the need to be even more careful about letting his real thoughts emerge. He now knows what happens when he speaks, and he clearly distrusts the media. He now knows that if he had not made flippant comments about the White House visit at a golf outing, there probably would not have been the ensuing furor.

While he hopes he has many more years of football, it probably won't be until it's over where he can fully engage his passions: His love of old people born out of his close relationship with his grandmother and his work as a dietary aide at a senior citizen complex while in college. His desire to help youngsters seeking football and life skills as well as a financial boost. His love of pets.

"Three things you can't go wrong with – old people, animals and kids. Old people are stuck in their ways and don't beat around the bush, kids have no filter and animals don't know any better," he says in admiration.

His easy relationships with kids no doubt stems from the horde of children at his house throughout childhood. "He'd come home and there'd always be little kids there," his mother says, either from one of his siblings or others his mom babysat.

Whatever the reasons, kids have always held a special place in his heart. He was never happier than after James III, a beautiful and rambunctious boy, was born in 2007. When Harrison is with his son, his carefully managed shield immediately drops. There is the hulking linebacker changing diapers. There he is watching cartoons with the child, wiping the kid's nose, playfully saying, "Let me get that booger. Let me get it," or bouncing James III on his knee. There he is pasting loving kisses on his son, the passionate shout of "Peace" when the child is taken to bed for the night.

There is nothing in this world Harrison loves more than his child, unless of course, it is the second child expected in late 2009. The man known for toughness says meekly: "When he comes into my arms, I want to cry."

Like his parents, Harrison is intent on being there for his kids. "When I grew up, I didn't get everything I wanted, but now I'm in a situation I can give him everything he needs and everything he wants. When he says: 'Daddy, I want to go here and here, Disney,' whatever it may be, I can take him there," says Harrison.

While his children are immensely important to him, it was an encounter with the baby's mother in February 2007 that nearly caused Harrison's life to be derailed after he reached success, as it so often had in the past.

Shortly after the birth of James III, Harrison set up a baptism at his grandmother's church. It was a snowy day when Harrison went to the home of Beth Tibbott, the baby's mother, in Ohio Township to pick up his son for the two-hour drive to Akron.

While Tibbott had agreed to the baptism, a snow storm hit Pittsburgh, causing Harrison to decide to leave a day early. Tibbott balked at that because she had family coming in from out of town.

That provoked an argument that quickly degenerated into a fight not only about the Baptism but also about what Harrison considered his diminished role in parental decisions. As the argument escalated, Harrison said Tibbott locked herself in her room and said she was calling police. He broke through the door, ripped her phone from her hand and snapped it apart as she hit him repeatedly in the face. He initially threw her onto a bed to thwart the attacks, but slapped her with an open hand when she came at him again.

When police arrived, the report said Tibbott had "red marks" on her left cheek. Minutes later, Franklin Park police pulled Harrison over. He owned up to his actions and was arrested on simple assault and criminal mischief charges.

The arrest caused a furor in Steeler Nation because it was the third such incident in a relatively short time, an abnormal number for the Steelers, who pride themselves on a squeaky clean public image and have routinely released players who have had run-ins with the law. The other two players involved in domestic abuse cases – second-stringers Cedric Wilson and Najeh Davenport – were eventually cut.

Even Dan Rooney was drawn into the controversy when some complained that the team was using a double standard. "I know of the incidents," he said. "They are completely different. In fact, when I say we don't condone these things, we don't, but we do have to look at the circumstances that are involved with other players and things like that, so they're not all the same. What Jimmy Harrison was doing and how the incident occurred, what he was trying to do was really well worth it. He was doing something that was good. He wanted to take his son to get baptized where he lived. She said she didn't want to do it." Rooney's statement was met with rare harsh criticism, some suggesting he was rationalizing domestic abuse.

While most lawyers never let their clients speak publicly about pending charges, Harrison insisted on setting the record straight. His lawyer, Robert Del Greco, a prominent criminal defense attorney, delivered the message: "I initially told him that my advice was he not speak with any of the media nor that I speak with

James Sr. and Mildred Harrison display the Super Bowl XLIII replica rings their son bought for them.

any of the media, and he felt strongly that I convey his contrition and his regret regarding the incident," Del Greco said at a press conference. He then read Harrison's brief statement: "I should never have laid my hands on that woman. It was wrong. It won't happen again."

Harrison still takes full responsibility for his actions, just as he has throughout his life when he does wrong. A district justice dropped all charges after Harrison went through an anger management program. The child was baptized later. Harrison still maintains a relationship with Tibbott, who is pregnant with the second child expected in late 2009, another boy.

Tibbott was also at the center of another highly publicized event that could have had a dire outcome. It happened in late May 2009, just days after the Obama snub story had run its course. Harrison was only minutes from his house, having just left a workout at Power Train Institute when a neighbor stopped him to say something was going on at his house.

He arrived only a few minutes later to find a chaotic scene. His dog was lying in front of police officers in his driveway, which was marked by large amounts of blood. They asked him to secure the dog in his pen, then told him it had attacked his son, Tibbott and a massage therapist awaiting Harrison's return from his workout. All of them already were headed to the hospital by ambulance. They had few other details.

An enraged Harrison's first thought was to go into his house and get a gun. "I told police I was going to put the dog down right there," he said about the attack on his precious child. He backed off when police told him he'd get arrested if he did that.

Before he knew the details, he got a frantic call from Tibbott, who was so upset that he couldn't understand what she was saying. Then a paramedic got on the phone to tell him the dog had bitten his son in the groin area close to his femoral artery. Harrison knew what that meant because a lacerated femoral artery caused the 2008 death of Washington Redskins defensive back Shawn Taylor, who was shot during a robbery at his Miami home and bled to death before doctors could repair it.

That knowledge made him increasingly frantic as he sped to Children's Hospital in Lawrenceville to be with his son, thinking the worst. "They told me he might die if it hit the artery or lose his leg," Tibbott said through tears. Harrison found his nephew Dylan in the hospital waiting room and learned the dog bite was serious.

As he awaited news of his son's fate, Mike Tomlin called to comfort him and later helped contact hospital officials to secure information about the child's condition. Harrison said the seemingly endless hour and a half wait for information was tortuous. His nephew had already told him the child's injuries were bad. "I was tripping, thinking the worse, but trying to stay calm," he said. Finally, Harrison learned the bite, though serious, had not affected the artery. "The doctor told me the bite came within one centimeter of the femoral artery, but that he was fine after he sutured him up," Harrison said. He was filled with joy when he was brought into the hospital room to find his son asleep.

As it turned out, everyone was, although almost 200 sutures were needed to close the extensive wounds that left scars on all of them. How did it happen? Harrison had trained the 2 ½-year-old dog, Patron, to listen to anything he says. It did not listen to others. While Tibbott was friendly with Patron, Harrison had repeatedly told her and everyone around him not to let the dog out of his cage when he wasn't there.

On this warm, late May day, Tibbott, her sister and Harrison's masseuse had been playing with James III on his expansive yard as Patron looked on from behind a locked kennel fence in the one-acre yard. Tibbott became concerned because the dog had fluid pouring from an eye, and it appeared his water was stale and hot. So she let him out of the kennel and wiped his eyes out as she was getting ready to refill his water bowl.

After a few minutes, James III, fell down on the grass and started crying. That provoked the attack against the toddler, who was bitten in the groin area. After the dog bit the child, a frantic Tibbott pulled it away and threw her body on top of James III to shield him. As she lay across her child, the dog mauled her, causing wounds that required more than 100 stitches in the front of her body.

At that point, the massage therapist grabbed the hysterical child and ran up a small hill toward Harrison's fenced in pool where she was bitten on the thigh as she placed the bleeding child on the other side of the pool fence. Harrison said the dog continued to try to get to the child through the fence, biting at the baby's diaper as the terrified little boy screamed. Finally, Harrison's nephew Dylan heard the commotion and came out of the house to secure the child in the pool area, applying pressure to the wounds as they awaited an ambulance.

Local media heard the 911 call on police scanners and arrived along with paramedics.

By the time he got home, the only thing Harrison would offer the news people were explicit orders to stay off his property, keeping them in the street. Parise said he got more than 400 calls about the incident over the next week.

In the midst of this traumatic event, the Harrison single-mindedness —that tunnel vision that helped him overcome adversity on his rise in professional football – took over. "He was very focused. He said 'I need to do a, b, and c' to make sure his son's care was good. It was very calculated, no outward emotion, but I'm sure there was a lot going on inside, because he was very scared for his son," said Parise.

"When we walked into the hospital room with him, it was nothing but a loving father. He kissed that baby 72 million times. It was wonderful, it was tender, it was sincere," Parise said.

There was the problem of the dog. "James was going to kill the dog. It had just mutilated his son," Parise said. While he loved the animal, he did not want to give it the chance to harm another child. As the days passed, Harrison rethought his decision because he didn't believe the dog was inherently bad. Now he wanted to see if he could find someone with no kids who would take it.

First, Parise had the dog evaluated by professionals, who said the dog was amenable to retraining. Then Parise found a couple who agreed to work with it. They initially took the dog to retrain it and place it with someone without children. After getting to know Patron, the couple decided they "absolutely adored the dog and kept it," Parise said.

Unlike anything else he had experienced, the two events in the spring of 2009 – one goofy, the other scary – proved one thing for sure. Everything Harrison does gets media attention.

"He was a little surprised because it was so personal, and it was his son and he felt his privacy was invaded. He felt like the media should have given him a little more space," Parise said. The Internet bloggers hit the dog-biting as hard as they did the Obama snub. "They were writing about whether the Steelers were going to fine him, whether the NFL would suspend him," Parise said, "and I said 'Are you kidding? His dog bit someone.' "

22

The Kids
Are All Right

He melts every time his son gazes at him, and he is elated about having another one on the way. Kids have always reduced Harrison from the angry, violent football player to a playful teddy bear. But he prefers to do things for young people away from the public eye. There are the YMCA scholarships he doles out to underprivileged children from the Beaver Valley near Pittsburgh through his "James Harrison's Sacks for Kids" charity. He says it "gives them something that helps to keep them off the streets."

He says little about the warm cards and thank-you notes he receives but clearly likes to make a difference in young lives, like that of Kyle Jones of Beaver County. Thanking Harrison for providing him with a YMCA scholarship, Kyle wrote: "It will keep me out of trouble and out of the street and give me something to do ...you don't know how much I appreciate this."

He frequently spends time visiting kids in hospitals and supporting various organizations.

While he had some awful experiences at Coventry High School, in 2008 Harrison plopped down $7,000 to buy Nike football

shoes for his old Ohio team because a coach told him some players couldn't afford them. Asked why he would give money to a
school where he had to endure racist epithets and was arrested,
Harrison pointed out that he never had any problems with his
Coventry teammates. Everything bad that happened to him was
caused by adults. He did earmark all the money for player shoes,
letting the coaches get their own.

This rarely seen compassion also emerged in his encounters
with kids during autograph sessions at off-season Steelers charity basketball events. On a March night in a sold-out gymnasium
at Union High School near New Castle, a large crowd formed at
halftime for Harrison's autograph. People were jostling and pushing to get there first. It was so crowded, he would sign only one
item per person.

Harrison tried to get people to wait their turn but to no avail.
That's when he looked up to see a middle-aged woman wedging
herself in front of a little kid patiently waiting in line. Harrison
looked past the line-cutter and addressed the kid, whose eyes
bugged out at the sight of his Steeler hero talking to him.

"Little man, come on now. You come up here," Harrison said.
As the child sidled up, his eyes showed the fear Harrison nor-
mally instills in opposing quarterbacks.

"Would you sign my shirt?" the shy child peeped.

"Yes, sir. There you go little man," he said as he not only signed
the shirt but a hat, too, even though he had refused requests for
a second autograph. "Thank you," the kid said meekly of an encounter he would likely never forget. "You are welcome," replied
a smiling Harrison.

A minute later, he stared down the middle-aged woman with
two Steelers shirts and a hat she wanted signed: "One per person," was his curt response.

Then there was the little girl who Harrison befriended during
one of the rare appearances he makes for the Muscular Dystro-
phy Foundation because it involves kids and he doesn't have
to give speeches. In 2006, he met a wheel-chair bound child,

bonded with her and agreed to come back the following year. While he agreed to go, his arrest occurred just days before, so he did not think it prudent to attend. When the saddened child wrote him, he made sure to go back to the 2008 event, which made the child's day.

Todd Murgatroyd, one of his college linebacker coaches, says Harrison had the same scowl on the football field at Kent as he does now, which scared many. Then one day he invited the linebackers to his home for a cookout. Harrison came with the other players, but as soon as he saw Murgatroyd's 2-year-old daughter and her tiny Shih Tzu dog, he was rolling on the floor with them. "I can still see him wrestling with her and the dog in my living room," he said.

Murgatroyd laughed when he recalled how his wife also fell for Harrison. She'd be sitting in the stands telling everyone how Harrison was " 'the sweetest thing in the whole wide world.' She'd tell everyone around her that James was such a nice, humble person, always saying 'Yes, ma'am, No, ma'am,' and then James would just whack someone," laughs Murgatroyd. He said that's when he realized Harrison was a pushover with animals and kids and folks like his wife – until he "puts a helmet on, and then he's not a nice guy."

Pees, then head coach at Kent, said Harrison also built relationships with his kids. Last summer, Harrison was at Cedar Point with his family when he encountered one of Pees' daughters. They talked about old times, and the coach's daughter called her dad who was staying nearby, and all of them enjoyed a brief reunion later that day.

Mike Archer, his first professional linebacker coach with the Steelers, said his children still tell stories about their relationships with Harrison. "I'd have the players out to my house when my kids were in high school. They loved him," he said. While the players would mill about talking, Harrison would be playing with the kids.

Parise said all you have to do to find out about Harrison's heart is to put him in a group of 20 kids. "He's warm, the warmest man you've ever seen," he said. "Bring him to a room of 20 kids. Watch him. He's the Pied Piper. He has a passion for kids, there's no doubt about it."

EPILOGUE

The Long
and Winding Road

There are all kinds of negatives about football players and other professional athletes when their careers end. High divorce rates. Once highly paid athletes now broke. Traumatic injuries that plague them the rest of their lives.

There are stories after stories about people like James Harrison who possess a never-say-die attitude on their field of dreams which bring them glory and financial riches. But when the cheering stops many can't recapture that feeling, despite sometimes spending their fortunes trying.

It would be easy to think an inner-city kid like Harrison could fall into the same trap.

So how does Harrison, the man whose singular focus in life did not allow him to give up his professional football dream, overcome those odds? For sure, Harrison, Parise and LeBeau believe he has the ability, stamina and will power to play another five to seven years, which would give him more than a dozen in the NFL with all of the money and glory that goes with it. But there is no doubt that by the time Harrison turns 40, like everyone else who straps on a helmet, it will be over.

Parise, a keen judge of character who has seen more than one of his clients end up broke, says Harrison's basic beliefs set him apart. In fact, Parise believes Harrison's unbending credo that brought him to the pinnacle of professional football will enable him to be successful off the gridiron.

It is a creed that Harrison has shown is hard to live by and is fraught with the controversy that has marked his life off and on since childhood. This way of life is not very complicated, but as Parise concedes, is not easy to follow for anyone not as focused as Harrison. In other words, unless you're extremely stout of heart, don't try this at home.

Most of these values have emerged anecdotally in this book, but when taken together they form a philosophy of life that has hurt and helped Harrison become who he is.

The first element: Tell the truth. Don't lie to people, and if you say something, always say exactly what you mean, something that rarely happens in today's world. Harrison's blunt answers are often threatening by any measure – and sometimes his brutal honesty is not very nice. But once he states his position, it's done. He doesn't mince words. He cuts to the chase. It is what it is. He rarely regrets speaking his mind, even if it has an outcome that hurts him.

The second part of the Harrison doctrine: Admit mistakes. Whether it's a BB gun battle in high school that would change his course in life, missing class in college, not immediately embracing coaches and their philosophies, or facing the fallout following a domestic abuse case, Harrison has never backed away from the truth or from admitting mistakes, even when it brings him down. It is also something his mother ingrained in him when he was very young. When he knows he's wrong, he says it, whether to a coach, a friend or a cop.

The third part of the Harrison approach is a persistent need to turn a weakness into a strength. He has had to deal with his shortcomings on the football field, in classrooms and in life with the same resolve he used to catapult himself from an undrafted free agent to NFL stardom. That resolve goes way back, too. He failed first grade, was called stupid or unwilling to pay the price in the classroom, but when he faced football extinction, he turned this Achilles' heel into a strong muscle by overcoming his non-qualifier status out of high school to earning honor roll status at Kent.

In the weight room, he was never a 150-pound weakling, but he has methodically – and painfully – built his body into a hulking mass that has made him one of the strongest men in the league and increased his speed and quickness through incredibly demanding workouts. Harrison was told he was so distant, uncoachable, even menacing to those around him that it caused him to be cut from NFL rosters four times. When he got his final chance, Harrison opened up his personality. He not only immersed himself in study to learn every linebacker's position but also showed his coaches he was a team player, that the only ones who should fear him are those on the opposite side of the ball.

The "want-to" factor has always been a pathway to success, and no one has that kind of push like James Harrison has shown again and again. Yes, he bounced around high schools in Ohio, but he wanted so badly to pursue higher education he overcame formidable odds to make it. Yes, he wasted his time when he started at Kent, risking failure, but again he decided he wanted to play football so badly that he buckled down in the classroom and on the field.

There is no greater sign of his overwhelming desire to succeed than overcoming four cuts to make it in the NFL. It didn't stop with the triumphant Super Bowl. While he was involved in almost every play during one quarter in the meaningless first preseason game of 2009, he voiced disappointment in his performance. "I'm now on a different level," he told Parise. "People expect more from me now."

One of the hardest things for Harrison to summon from his heart is trust. He admits he trusts no one implicitly, but he has a close circle of friends and family who have either earned it by building it or by circumstances of birth. Over the years, he has softened on that issue, as his mind has opened to a degree, showing he is not only willing to change, but also to grow and believe in others, such as the immortal Dick LeBeau, his defensive coordinator, to whom Harrison pays his ultimate compliment: "I trust him."

All of these beliefs are part and parcel of what have made Harrison one of the most feared and now the best defensive player in the best football league in the world. But they sit below the single article of faith that has guided Harrison in life and in football:

Never give up.

Harrison's Statistics

James Harrison
Pittsburgh Steelers (sixth year)

Height:. **6-0**

Weight:. **250**

Born:. . . . .**May 4, 1978**

College:. . . . . **Kent State**

Major:. . . . .**General Studies**

High School:. . . . . . . **Coventry (Akron, Ohio)**

James enjoying himself while in Hawaii for the Pro Bowl.

Career Statistics
Pittsburgh Steelers

	Games	Starts	Tackles			Sacks	Safeties	Deflection	Inteceptions	Fumbles
			Total	Solo	Assists					
2008	15	15	101	67	34	16	1	3	1 for 33 yds	1
2007	16	16	98	76	22	8.5		3	1 for 20 yds	
2006	11	1	20	14	6					
2005	16	3	45	36	9	3		3	1 for 25 yds	
2004	16	4	45	36	9	1		2		
2002	1									
Total	75	39	309	229	80	28.5	1	11	3 for 78 yds	1

Harrison is flanked by fellow Pro Bowlers Troy Polamalu (left) and James Farrior (right) at the 2009 Pro Bowl.

College Statistics

Kent State

Games	Tackles	Tackles for Loss	Sacks	Interceptions	Fumbles
1999	67	9			
2000	106	13	3	1	3
2001	98	20	12	3	3

Harrison stands proud with his AFC teammates at the 2009 Pro Bowl.

James and Linda Parise at the Pro Bowl 2009

Harrison and Kurt Warner of the Arizona Cardinals get interviewed by NBC about the 100-yard interception return for a touchdown at the 2009 Pro Bowl.

Acknowledgements

I would like to thank everyone who helped with the creation of this book. The list includes Jim Wexell, who gave a guy he didn't know advice and counsel; Ed Bouchette of the Pittsburgh Post-Gazette, Mike McGinley, Art Rooney II and Diane Lowe of the Steelers; Marie Do Rego and Matt Stroud, who picked up the slack at the Innocence Institute of Point Park University while I worked; Leah Moushey for lining up the business end of things before she left for Syracuse University, along with Wil, who helped out before heading to Albany N.Y. for football camp; Ross Morgan Jr. and his Pitt friends who distributed book marks all over town; Leslie, Rachel and Jessica Moushey, along with Jean Saunders, who alerted folks all over the globe about this work; Judy and Dave Bauer who told everyone they knew about it; to Christopher Rand and Jackie Costa, the Myrtle Beach connection; to John Nubani of Sports Management and Marketing Inc., and to my wife Kris, who is always my helping hand. Finally, this could not have been done without the careful, thoughtful edit by the great Peter Leo, the man known as "Strength" during his many years in the newsroom of the Pittsburgh Post-Gazette where he was the best columnist ever on what used to be "One of America's Great Newspapers;" Helen Fallon, who put a final copy edit on the project; Catherine Tigano Gianella, who brought life to the work with a wonderful design, and her cousin Janet Lea, who repeatedly offered a helping artistic hand. I will forever be grateful to all of you as well as many others unmentioned here who helped make my dream of publishing a book come true. *— B.M.*